Sowing the Seed of Truth

Orthodox Quaker Sermons
of Murray Shipley (1873–1876)

Edited by Sabrina Darnowsky
Foreword by Thomas D. Hamm

Murray Shipley, born March 1, 1830, New York, NY; died January 20, 1899, Cincinnati, OH. Courtesy of The Shipley School, Bryn Mawr, PA.

[It] is our duty to go forth and sow the seed as the Lord may direct us, but our dependence is on God who causes the seed sown "to grow up." It is not that we impart the Holy Ghost, but that to our hand is entrusted the sowing of the seed of truth.

— MURRAY SHIPLEY, MARCH 18, 1876

Copyright 2024 by Sabrina Darnowsky

All rights reserved. No portion of this book may be reproduced, stored in electronic retrieval system or transmitted in any form or by means—electronic, mechanical, photocopy, recording or other—except for brief quotations in printed reviews, without the permission of the publisher.

Cover photograph courtesy of The Shipley School, Bryn Mawr, PA.

Photograph of Sabrina Darnowsky (p. 131) by Dianne Bomar, www.TheNewStudio.net

Book design by David Botwinik

Library of Congress Cataloging-in-Publication Data
Names: Darnowsky, Sabrina, editor.
Title: Sowing the Seed of Truth : Orthodox Quaker Sermons of Murray Shipley (1873-1876) / Sabrina Darnowsky ; foreword by Thomas D. Hamm.
Description: Richmond, IN : Friends United Press, 2024. | Includes bibliographical references and index.
Identifiers: LCCN 2023056575 (print) | LCCN 2023056576 (ebook) | ISBN 9781956149272 (hardback) | ISBN 9781956149258 (trade paperback) | ISBN 9781956149265 (epub)
Subjects: LCSH: Society of Friends--Sermons.
Classification: LCC BX7733.S55 S695 20024 (print) | LCC BX7733.S55 (ebook) | DDC 252/.096—dc23/eng/20240125
LC record available at https://lccn.loc.gov/2023056575
LC ebook record available at https://lccn.loc.gov/2023056576

Friends United Press
101 Quaker Hill Drive
Richmond, IN 47374
friendsunitedmeeting.org

ISBN 978-1-956149-25-8 (paperback)
      978-1-956149-26-5 (ebook)
      978-1-956149-27-2 (hardcover)

CONTENTS

FOREWORD by Thomas D. Hamm vii

PREFACE ix
    About Shipley's Journal x
    About This Book xii

INTRODUCTION xv
    About Murray Shipley xix

CHAPTER 1 *Personal Anecdotes* 1
    [Drawn to Christ] 2
    [Hidden Treasure] 3
    [Our Father's Mercy Seat] 4
    [Sowing the Seed] 6

CHAPTER 2 *Dramatic Narratives* 8
    Follow Me 10
    He Healed Them All 13
    [My Father's Business] 15
    [Atonement] 18
    This Man Receiveth Sinners 23
    Lovest Thou Me. Feed My Sheep. Follow Me 29

CHAPTER 3 *Parables, Allegories, and Analogies* 32
    [Discovering the Ever-Present] 34
    Rights of Heavenly Citizenship 35
    [Expecting and Realizing] 37
    Yield 41
    Grace 42
    Invisible 44
    Direct 47

CONTENTS

CHAPTER 4 *Current Events and Social Reform* 51
    [By Faith and Not by Sight] 53
    [Supplying Every Need] 55
    [Tribulation] 56
    Who Went About Doing Good 58

CHAPTER 5 *Explications* 64
    [Knowledge and Power] 66
    Separation 69
    [Holiness] 72
    [The Love of God] 74
    Expectation 76
    [Trust] 77
    [Building Up] 81

CHAPTER 6 *Exhortation* 86
    [Loving the Lord] 88
    [Not Ashamed] 92
    [No Difference] 94
    Repentance 95

CHAPTER 7 *Eulogies* 97
    On the Death of John Sensenny 99
    On the Death of Rachel Balderston (Stokes) 102
    Hannah Wilson's Funeral 103

NOTES 107

BIBLIOGRAPHY 121
    Murray Shipley's Bibliography 121
    The Author's Bibliography 122

ACKNOWLEDGMENTS 126

INDEX 128

ABOUT SABRINA DARNOWSKY 131

ABOUT THOMAS D. HAMM 131

FOREWORD

Sabrina Darnowsky has done a service to scholars of Quakerism and, we can hope, to spiritual inquirers as well in providing us with this published version of the sermons of Murray Shipley. Now largely forgotten, Shipley was a well-known, generally respected, and, at times, controversial figure among members of the Religious Society of Friends on both sides of the Atlantic from the 1860s until his death.

As Sabrina Darnowsky notes in her introduction, Quaker preaching in this period presents us with problems. Since the inception of their Religious Society in the 1650s, Friends had strongly believed that all ministry or speaking in meetings for worship must be under the direct inspiration of the Holy Spirit. By the eighteenth century, Friends had hardened this belief into a conviction that to give *any* forethought to what one might say in a meeting was to "get ahead of the Guide" and "creaturely," evidence that one was proceeding according to one's own will rather than waiting for a divine leading. The result is that while we have many accounts of Quaker preaching in the letters of individual Friends—both preachers and hearers—the exact sermons themselves are lost. The published Quaker sermons we do have before the late nineteenth century were invariably the work of enterprising printers, never Quakers, who sensed an interest in the preaching of a particular Friend and sent someone with shorthand abilities into Friends meetings to take down what was said. The earliest such collection was published in London in 1694.[1] The printing of the sermons of Elias Hicks and their circulation was one of the primary drivers of the Hicksite Separation among American Friends in the 1820s.[2]

In the early 1870s, however, Shipley—already a well-respected recorded minister among Friends—began making notes about his preaching. We don't know if they reflect his thoughts before he went to meeting, or whether they are notes that he made afterwards; the latter seems more likely. But they give us an almost unique glimpse of the preaching of admirers of the English minister Joseph John Gurney. Gurneyite Friends, including Shipley, made up the largest of the strains of American Quakerism that emerged after 1820. We can only regret that Shipley did not begin writing down his messages earlier and continue longer. His sermon manuscripts do not answer some questions that we would love to have answered. In 1875 Shipley became a center of major controversy when, on a visit to the British Isles, he felt led to undergo water baptism, a practice that Friends traditionally considered a spiritual rather than physical experience. His sermons mention no reasons for this action nor his response to the criticism he received as a result. His manuscripts likewise do not explain why Shipley, who was identified with the Revivalist party among Gurneyite Friends before 1875, later came to have reservations about the radical innovations that Friends like David B. Updegraff, a Quaker minister from Mt. Pleasant, Ohio, were introducing into Friends meetings, including the idea of instantaneous sanctification.

Still, we should be grateful for what we do have. Sabrina Darnowsky deserves our gratitude for making these manuscripts available and expertly delineating their historical, biographical, and spiritual context.

Thomas D. Hamm
EMERITUS PROFESSOR OF HISTORY AND
QUAKER SCHOLAR IN RESIDENCE, EARLHAM COLLEGE

PREFACE

For individuals who want to delve into the historic thought and theology of members of the Religious Society of Friends (more commonly known as Quakers), there have always been ample resources, including such classics as the journal of the seventeenth-century English Quaker pioneer George Fox; Robert Barclay's defense of Quakerism in *An Apology for the True Christian Divinity*; William Penn's devotional work *No Cross, No Crown*; and the journal of the American abolitionist and pacifist John Woolman. Popular nineteenth-century periodicals such as *The Friend* and *Friends' Review* provided forums for discussing contemporary issues, and a plethora of Quaker pamphlets covered subjects ranging from the divine mysteries to advice for children. The William H. Jenks collection at Haverford College alone contains more than 1,500 tracts, booklets, and other materials written between the mid-seventeenth and nineteenth centuries.

Studying Quaker preaching, however, is a more daunting task. Friends have traditionally eschewed maintaining a written record of their messages, as noted by the minister William Savery in 1797:

> It is not my practice, nor that of my fellow-labourers in our religious society, to bring to our Meetings any thing prepared for communication; but we believe it right, to resign our minds to the will and direction of Him, in whom are hid all the treasures of wisdom and knowledge; and who still, from time to time, graciously influences the hearts and tongues of his servants, to publish salvation in the immediate revelation of his power....
>
> It has greatly added to the exercise which some have felt, under the weight of the awful service in which they have been engaged, to find, that many of their declarations have been attempted to be written down in Short-hand, and some of them printed;—a practice, which I believe not only they, but the solid part of our religious society, disapprove.[1]

The Quaker historian and Earlham College emeritus professor Thomas D. Hamm has observed that almost no Orthodox Quaker sermon manuscripts from the mid-nineteenth century have survived, which limits any insights into what was being said in worship during an exceptionally turbulent period in American Quaker history.[2] So it was a rare find indeed to discover a collection of roughly fifty-eight sermons penned by a Cincinnati minister, Murray Shipley, between 1873 and 1876, adding to our knowledge of that period.

About Shipley's Journal

When he was forty-three years old and had been a minister for five years,[3] Murray Shipley obtained a 9 x 14-inch bound blank book with 282 ruled and numbered pages, similar to the record books used by his Quaker meeting for its business minutes. He filled the first dozen or so pages with systematic notes from his studies of the Bible, typically focusing on a single word like *comfort* or *riches*, and then writing a long list of scriptures that contained that word, forming his own personal concordance. Sometimes he expressed a few of his own thoughts on the subject; at other times he included quotations from the work of prominent Protestant preachers and scholars, demonstrating his own evangelical ecumenism. Eventually, he began writing out his own sermons.

Nearly half of the sermons included the date and occasionally the place and time when the message was given. It is uncertain whether the undated sermons were not delivered or were simply not identified in the same way as the others. Of those that were geographically labeled, nine were delivered in Cincinnati; three in New Burlington, Ohio (about fifty miles north of Cincinnati); and one in Newport, Rhode Island. In the late spring of 1874, Shipley and several members of his family began a stay in Kendal, England, that lasted more than a year.[4] While overseas he preached several sermons in Kendal; one each in Darlington, Kent, and Liverpool, England; and one possibly in Switzerland.

The majority of his messages were delivered on Sunday, presumably during morning worship, although several were given on weekdays, possibly at a mid-week or evening meeting. Others, however, were shared at venues outside of worship. The message in Darlington was given at a First-Day School Conference, and one in Kendal was at the Kendal Mission Meeting.

Although Shipley stated that he sought to deliver his messages "as [God] sees is suited and suitable at the time," the chronology of his journal suggests that he at least occasionally broke with the old Quaker tradition of impromptu preaching and wrote down his messages in advance. For example, the first sermon in his journal has a delivery date of March 14, 1875, while the next one with a date was given on May 26, 1873, indicating that his first sermon may have been written about two years before it was spoken. He even delivered one particular sermon on two separate occasions: once in Cincinnati, Ohio, on June 1, 1873, and again in Kendal, England, on June 10, 1874. This sidestepped a longstanding Quaker injunction against reusing sermon material, lest it not meet the immediate needs of the moment.[5] The last date given to a sermon was October 30, 1876.[6]

Shipley was not alone in taking a more premeditated approach to preaching. One of his contemporaries, Allen Jay, strongly endorsed the idea:

> [Avoiding the use of notes while speaking] does not prevent study beforehand. It does not mean that the sermon shall not be written out and thought over and the mind filled with it. On the other hand, it makes it more necessary. Then, from a well-filled storehouse let the Spirit draw out things new and old. It may require the burning of midnight oil to prepare the sermon, but let the Spirit so permeate it that it will take all the smell of the oil out of it.[7]

Although Shipley appeared to write at least some of his messages in advance, his memorial minute nevertheless notes that the "reverent attitude which he assumed upon taking his seat in our meetings was very observable, as it was always his practice to wait upon the Lord in silent worship before any vocal service. He often opened the meeting with earnest thanksgiving and prayer."[8]

Despite periodic deviations from historical preaching practices, Shipley shared with early Quaker ministers a common desire: to turn his listeners toward God and encourage them to lead pure and loving lives, not because of religious tradition or outward dictates, but because of an inner transformation that resulted from a direct experience of the divine.

About This Book

This book includes an introduction to the central tenets of Quakerism and how they affected early Friends' approach to preaching, an overview of the changes that occurred in the Religious Society of Friends in the nineteenth century, and the perspectives offered by Murray Shipley's ministry in particular.

The rest of the book contains edited transcriptions of thirty-five of the sermons that appear in Shipley's journal. These messages are organized into chapters that reflect their distinguishing rhetorical characteristics:

- Anecdotes from his own personal experiences
- Dramatic narratives based on Bible stories, imagined figures from Biblical times, and contemporary characters
- Parables, allegories, and analogies that expand on those of Jesus or reflect the culture and technologies of his own time
- Reactions to current events and encouragement to engage in social reform
- Explications of terms or concepts
- Exhortations to take certain actions, such as talking about spiritual matters in the home
- Eulogies

Of course, not all of Shipley's sermons fall neatly into such categories. *Direct* is a tour-de-force that demonstrates several preaching techniques: the implicitly personal experience of watching a gondolier navigate the canals in Venice, the dramatization of the story of the prodigal son, and the contemporary references to the Civil War, the country's economic instability, and the social institutions of his time. But ultimately, his closing words return to the image of the gondola, thus putting this sermon in the chapter on parables, allegories, and analogies.

Less than half of the sermons in Shipley's journal had titles; the rest were distinguishable as separate messages based on where the writing on the previous page ended, or a change in topic. When no title was given, I provided one, enclosed in square brackets.

Shipley typically prefaced each sermon with one or more Bible verses. In instances where the list was extensive, I reduced the citations to those that seemed most salient to his message. Likewise, to avoid disrupting the flow of his narrative, I did not include lengthy lists of scriptures or other asides that were occasionally interspersed in the rest of the sermon.

Like all ministers during this period, Shipley used the King James Version of the Bible. In instances where he appeared to intentionally truncate or paraphrase verses, or when he added a clarifying parenthetical, I let his wording stand. Where there were minor omissions, word transpositions, or spelling errors, I corrected the quotation to match the source. Likewise, direct quotations from the printed works of other ministers were amended as necessary to match the original. I retained the scripture citations for all introductory verses and those where Shipley explicitly referred to the source in his text (such as "As we read Romans 3"). For other citations, both those he added as parentheticals in his text and those where the verse was quoted but not directly attributed, the verse appears in the end notes.

Shipley's journal was handwritten and significantly marked up with editorial revisions. I take full responsibility for misreading any of his words. His use of capitalization was inconsistent, and his punctuation sometimes scant or ambiguous. To make his text easier for contemporary readers to follow, I took the liberty of occasionally inserting paragraph breaks, dividing extremely long sentences into shorter ones, adding clarifying punctuation where needed, and correcting grammatical and spelling errors rather than inserting [sic]. When a word or phrase was clearly inadvertently omitted or misspoken, when the handwriting was illegible, or when shorthand references appeared in lieu of text, I added what seemed to be his intention in square brackets. Words and phrases that Shipley underlined in his journal appear in italic.

With these enhancements, I hope that anyone interested in Quaker preaching, historic doctrine among Friends, or comparative religion can discover insights into the theology of this nineteenth-century Orthodox Quaker minister, the rhetorical techniques that he used to communicate his gospel message, and the period in which he lived.

A page from Murray Shipley's journal. Courtesy of Haverford College, Quaker & Special Collections, Haverford, PA.

INTRODUCTION

Since its formation in the latter half of the seventeenth century, the Religious Society of Friends has upheld the idea that God has given a measure of divine Light to all people, who can either resist it or yield to it. Those who yield can be taught and led by the Spirit, just as the first-century apostles and disciples were. "I directed all to the Spirit of God in themselves," wrote the early Quaker leader George Fox, "that they might be turned from darkness to Light, and believe in it; that they might become the children of it, and might . . . all come to know Christ to be their teacher to instruct them."[1] This reliance on direct revelation infuses all Quaker practices, including their approach to preaching.[2]

From the beginning, Friends abandoned the formal lectionary and liturgy that structured worship in the Church of England and other dissenting religious movements of the time, such as Puritanism. Theological education itself was regarded skeptically as more vocational training than a religious calling. Fox quipped that "being bred at Oxford or Cambridge did not qualify or fit a man to be a minister of Christ."[3] Mere knowledge was no substitute for a personal experience of the divine presence. If the still, small voice of God was indeed still speaking to humankind, then worship must involve listening—quieting the body and mind, and waiting upon the Lord. From the depth of that silence, any person—male or female, young or old—might feel the Spirit stirring the waters of their soul and pour out a message. Such a message was not a speech prepared in advance, but rather an impromptu response to an immediate spiritual leading.[4]

Although anyone could provide this type of vocal ministry, by the 1730s Quakers began officially noting that certain individuals had a particular calling to it. This acknowledgement process was known as *recording*.[5] It was not equivalent to ordination; it was simply the recognition of a person's gift from God—freely received, freely to be given. The few prerequisites for becoming a recorded minister included demonstrating evidence of personal sanctification and upright behavior, divine inspiration, a right understanding of the things of God as professed by Friends, and humility.[6]

While the sermons of Anglican and Puritan priests and ministers were singularly focused, systematic discourses on doctrine and Biblical explication, those of Quaker ministers were often a mosaic of different themes: the universal need of salvation; God's love for humankind; justification through Christ's blood; the importance of loving others, self-denial, and moral purity; and the possibility of perfection (living in the absence of sin). Their messages also occasionally reiterated ideas that were particularly important to Friends: the spiritual rather than physical nature of baptism and communion, simplicity in living, honesty in business, refusal to take oaths or pay compulsory tithes to the state church, adherence to "plain language" (using *thee* and *thou* with all people rather than using *you* for individuals of higher social status), and opposition to war.[7]

Early generations of Quaker ministers also took a different approach to using scriptures in their preaching. Rather than beginning with a Biblical text and expounding on it, they typically spoke first of a direct personal revelation or inspiration, and then supported it with scripture. Of course, to be able to cite scripture, Quaker ministers had to be familiar with it. Studying and memorizing the Bible was a natural part of their devotional life, and at that time it was considered the only acceptable form of preparation for speaking.[8]

Yet scriptural reinforcement was not the only measure of a message's truth. Those Friends hearing a minister's words pour forth were not merely empty receptacles but active filters, listening for that of God during worship and then later offering the minister encouragement or gentle correction as needed.[9] Indeed, stubbornly resisting the instruction of others was considered evidence of a self-deluded soul.[10]

This approach to preaching continued largely unchanged for many decades. However, during the nineteenth century, several upheavals in the Religious Society of Friends shifted the trajectory of Quaker ministry in America.

In the late 1820s, a bitter schism occurred over the preaching of the itinerant minister Elias Hicks. Like seventeenth-century Friends, Hicks believed deeply in direct revelation and relying on guidance from the Inward Light. However, where Hicks raised hackles among his fellow Quakers was in his emphasis on the human nature of the historical Jesus, his perspective that Jesus was the son of God in the same sense that all people are God's children, and his questioning the need of a blood sacrifice for the forgiveness of sins.[11] Although Hicks based some of his assertions on his reading of scripture and spoke of the importance of understanding scriptures rightly, he also expressed the idea that the Bible was a cause of division and sectarianism. "It has divided [Christendom] into hundreds of sects, all fixing their foundation upon this literal book as though it were a sufficient rule," expounded Hicks. "And so long as it is considered so, there may be hundreds of thousands [of sects], for everyone can put on a new construction and give it a different interpretation."[12] In his sermons, Hicks tested the boundaries of what was considered acceptable discourse in Quaker preaching.

The pushback from those who held a more traditionally Protestant understanding of their faith, who labeled themselves *Orthodox*, was vigorous. Several of the yearly meetings—the larger organizations responsible for making decisions regarding doctrine and practice for their constituent local meetings—splintered apart. For example, where there once was just one body known as Indiana Yearly Meeting that encompassed Quakers in western Ohio, Indiana, and Illinois, there was now an Indiana Yearly Meeting of Orthodox Friends and an Indiana Yearly Meeting of Hicksite Friends.[13] At the local meeting level, Orthodox Friends began purging their membership rolls of anyone who aligned with or was simply sympathetic toward Hicks, including their own ministers.[14]

Beginning in the late 1830s, Orthodox Quakers in America were also deeply influenced by a charismatic and scholarly English preacher, Joseph John Gurney. Like early Friends, Gurney valued silent worship and the traditional approach toward ministry.

xvii

However, he differed from his spiritual ancestors in several key ways. Gurney elevated the importance of the Bible over direct revelation. He emphasized the idea that justification was a separate, instantaneous experience that came through the simple expression of faith in Christ, although he continued to maintain the traditional Quaker understanding that sanctification was a gradual process. Gurney also worked toward cutting a gap through the "hedge" that Quakers had planted around themselves, separating themselves from others with their peculiar manner of dress and speech as well as their distinctive attitudes about sacraments and peace. He encouraged Friends to interact with other denominations on benevolent work and thus to find common ground with members of other evangelical Protestant faiths.[15]

Inspired by Gurney, in the 1860s a cadre of relatively young Quaker leaders turned their attention toward what they saw as the spiritual stagnation within their Religious Society. In some meetings, worship had become excessively silent as a result of heavy-handed Elders. These individuals were appointed by a meeting to attend to its spiritual well-being, offering counsel and guidance to ministers and other members when needed. However, some Elders vigorously frowned upon vocal ministry that they did not consider sound, to the point that only those who were recorded ministers or on the path to becoming recorded were inclined to speak. Friends who did speak occasionally exhibited odd patterns that had for some time characterized Quaker preaching—the prefacing of each sentence with a distinct sigh, an almost chanting intonation, and an erratic delivery as the speaker paused abruptly for the next divinely inspired word.[16]

The galvanized reformers encouraged all Friends to share their religious convictions and experiences during worship. They likewise urged Quaker ministers to adopt a more systematic approach to Bible study—including the use of outside aids by other Protestant theologians and commentators—to help them better understand scriptural truths and avoid eccentric interpretations in their preaching.[17]

Among these reformers was Murray Shipley.[18]

INTRODUCTION

About Murray Shipley

Murray Shipley was born in 1830 in New York City to a family with deep Quaker roots in Uttoxeter, England, and the American colonies.[19] His paternal grandmother, Ann Shipley, was herself a recorded minister who was very highly regarded.[20] In 1824 when she wrote a letter defending her English friend Anna Braithwaite in a public dispute with Elias Hicks, Hicks's allies questioned the authenticity of the letter rather than Ann Shipley's reputation.[21] When the Hicksite separation occurred several years later, Murray Shipley's grandmother and his parents both aligned themselves with the Orthodox, as did Murray throughout his lifetime.[22]

Shipley came to Cincinnati with his parents and one of his half-sisters when he was twelve years old.[23] Decades later, looking back on his own spiritual journey, he echoed the sentiments of the introductory chapters of Ecclesiastes: all our own efforts to find fulfillment are in vain.

> As I grew up I took a survey of life. I thought I saw that riches gained happiness, but I found they were as ashes when obtained. I thought that in a prudent life laid happiness, but I soon learned that care corroded. I then thought that pleasure gained life, and I sought it in whatever would gratify, but I never found it there. I sought peace in a moral life. I tried it over and over again, giving up everything that seemed in the way. I ever saw written before me the spirituality of the first commandment. I then beheld the blood of Jesus, and heard the "Come unto me, all ye that are heavy laden, and I will give you rest." And I found rest in Jesus.[24]

In many ways, Shipley's approach to ministry presaged trends that would sweep through Quakerism during the last half of the nineteenth century. He was an early and enthusiastic adopter of evangelism outside of his Religious Society. Under his leadership in the late 1850s, Cincinnati Monthly Meeting began an ambitious effort to disseminate religious tracts throughout the city to all classes of citizens—merchants and mechanics as well as the infirm, the imprisoned, and the impoverished. Between November of 1859 and November of 1860, a committee of about a dozen Quakers handed out over 20,000 such tracts—more than one in ten Cincinnatians received the gospel message at the hand of Friends.²⁵

The autumn of 1860 was also the year that Shipley and a small group of other reformers in Indiana Yearly Meeting planned an unprecedented evening religious gathering in Richmond, Indiana, specifically for young people. It was not quite like the camp meetings that were proliferating among local Methodists, which typically featured extensive preaching, hymn singing, and chaotic outbursts of lamentations and prayers among the audience. The Quaker organizers of this event insisted that any ministers in attendance would not preach, lest they monopolize the time intended for young Friends to participate. There was no set format for the meeting, no urgings to speak, no call for converts, and only a single person attempted to sing. Yet one by one, more than 150 members of a crowd estimated at 1,000 people exclaimed their testaments of devotion until the early hours of the morning.²⁶

By the time Shipley was recorded as a minister in 1868, revival-style events were still uncommon among Friends.²⁷ Shipley himself possessed a calm, intellectual temperament,²⁸ yet he foresaw the potential in the revival movement to increase interest and enthusiasm within his Religious Society. In 1869, while traveling among the staid, traditionally conservative Friends of Pennsylvania, Shipley made the audacious move of using the kind of language and facilitating the kind of gathering that would later become typical among Quaker promoters of holiness.²⁹ William S. Taylor, the 22-year-old son of one of Shipley's cousins, wrote disparagingly of what he observed:

> Murray Shipley announced at the close of meeting last 1st day that "18 had *confessed* at Haverford." . . . I'd rather any day listen to a Methodist. I fully believe in *true* worship, faith in the Savior, and the leading of a life as genuine Christians, but when a man . . . blows his horn to every one (the Pharisee's style) and says boldly in meeting "I *am saved*, I *know it*" . . . (the first Murray said right out and the last he clearly implied)—I can tell thee Charlie, it's disgusting. Murray's doctrine of "once in grace, always in grace" won't go down, it's false doctrine. Then he called all the young people together, stirred them to the highest pitch, got all to "confessing,"

down to his youngest "sprig" Morris, none hardly knowing what they were talking about and most of the females crying, but two days [later] most had forgotten, as they showed in meeting, what had been either said or done.

Such *revivals* as this are, I think, to say the least wicked. . . . I do *hate* [rant] and believe truly that the Devil has a good deal to do with it. Don't be led into Murray's, and every "progressive Friend's," style of "confessing," it will only make a *fool* of yourself and do *no one* any good.

A wild, crazy mania is far from true religion.[30]

Throughout the 1870s and beyond, revival meetings blew through Quaker communities like a rushing wind. Some Friends perceived it as a breath of fresh air; others found it more like a cyclone, leaving discord and disruption in its wake.[31] The interdenominational holiness movement had significantly influenced the Religious Society of Friends by the time Shipley began writing his journal in 1873, and he had close connections with several of its Quaker leaders.[32] Yet his sermons indicate that he did not embrace some of the contemporaneous tenets of holiness theology:

- Human beings were inherently wicked.[33]
- Sanctification came through an instantaneous second experience of grace after conversion.[34]
- Because Christ was expected to return at the turn of the century, saving souls should be the sole focus of ministry.[35]
- The traditional manner of Quaker worship was outmoded.[36]

There is no doubt that Shipley believed that all people were sinners in need of salvation. However, rather than seeing humans as fundamentally depraved, Shipley seemed to agree with early Friends that there was that of God in everyone, although he did not typically use traditional Quaker language in expressing it. Quoting the English theologian Julius Hare, Shipley noted that "unless there was a living principle in the plant, the warmth of the sun would no more unfold the blossoms, than it can open an artificial bud, or a painted one." In other words, without some flicker of Inward Light within the soul, without the living seed of Christ implanted in the heart, it would not be possible to respond to God's loving outreach. In reflecting on the human condition, Shipley often expressed compassion for those who were regarded as lowly sinners by genteel society, and scorn for those who held themselves in high regard for their own religiosity, morality, and philanthropy.

There is likewise no doubt that Shipley believed in the necessity of conversion—"a hearty turning away from the known sinfulness of your lives and from your own efforts to be good and looking up unto Jesus crucified for you," as he described the concept in his sermon *Expecting and Realizing*. However, in his journal Shipley never mentioned the need for a second experience, nor even used the word *sanctification* except once when quoting a Bible verse. He emphasized that an authentic experience of God would be transformative, and if he at one time proclaimed "once in grace, always in grace" as Taylor claimed, his sermons suggest a more nuanced view. Indeed, Shipley noted that a lack of transformation belied a lack of true obedience. In *Rights of Heavenly Citizenship*, he asserted that anyone who claimed to believe but did not yield to the will of God would "prove the argument for justice and not mercy."

For Shipley, the transformation wrought in the soul by God would find its expression in both increased personal virtue and active demonstrations of love toward others by making the world a better place. Thus, he rejected the premise of premillennialism—the idea that the world was inevitably becoming ever more evil in anticipation of the Second Coming. In both his sermons and his life, he upheld examples of ways to be God's hands in establishing His kingdom on earth. From founding The Children's Home which placed orphaned and abandoned youngsters into families, to managing a workingman's coffeehouse as an alternative to saloons, Shipley lived out Jesus's commandment to love your neighbor as yourself, and encouraged others to take up similar tasks.[37]

Although Shipley touted the transformation of the self and the world at large, he resisted the upheaval of Quaker worship practices advocated by holiness preachers. John Henry Douglas, who had stood quietly with Shipley at the 1860 gathering for young

INTRODUCTION

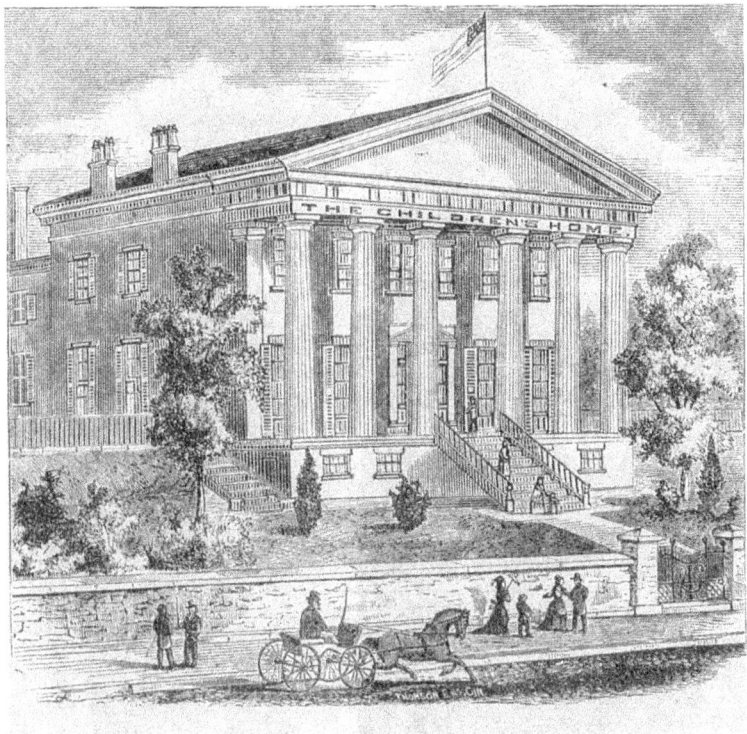

The Children's Home, Cincinnati, Ohio, c. 1871. Murray Shipley was a founder of the home which placed orphaned and abandoned children into families. Courtesy of the Cincinnati & Hamilton County Public Library.

people, would become known for holding up a Bible and offering his listeners $100 if they could show where that book said that worship should be silent.[38] After all, if God was always with the sanctified, what need was there to solemnly wait for the leading of the Spirit?[39]

There is no evidence that Shipley sought to replace expectant silence with extensive preaching and singing in worship. Most of his messages were quite brief, allowing ample time for quiet self-reflection and prayer. Although he occasionally quoted or alluded to popular hymns in his sermons, Cincinnati Monthly Meeting did not adopt singing during worship until 1900, after Shipley's death.[40] Shipley did share the revivalists' concern, however, that silent worship and other Quaker traditions should not become a "dead

Meetinghouse of Cincinnati Monthly Meeting, Eighth and Mound Streets, Cincinnati, Ohio. Murray Shipley was a member and a recorded minister of this meeting. Courtesy of Cincinnati Monthly Meeting.

form" that provided its practitioners with a false sense of spiritual security. Like early Friends, Shipley wanted his listeners to have a direct experience of the divine presence. He insisted that it was not enough to live the plain life, to sit in silence during worship, and to avoid the ordinances. For Shipley, true spirituality resided in a heart that melted at the glad tidings of the gospel, and a will that yielded to God's loving guidance. That was the seed of truth that he hoped to sow.

CHAPTER 1

Personal Anecdotes

In his eighteenth-century work *A Description of the Qualifications Necessary to a Gospel Minister*, Samuel Bownas encouraged his fellow Quaker ministers to "declare to others with power and authority, in the word of life, what God has done for our souls."[1] Shipley himself never described his own personal religious experiences in his sermons, but he did use moments from his life as illustrations for his messages.

Drawn to Christ is the first message in his journal in which Shipley describes a personal experience, implicitly comparing being drawn to a lit house in the woods at night to being drawn to the Light of God. Likewise, he describes a visit to a patient with consumption, who held his New Testament near to himself, just as we are to inwardly hold Christ near to ourselves.

In *Hidden Treasure*, he shares his experience of watching a deep-sea diver in Narragansett Bay off the coast of his summer home in Newport, Rhode Island, and likens such an action to an act of faith.

Our Father's Mercy Seat, which describes the reconciliation Shipley facilitated between an estranged husband and wife, reflects the possibilities of grace. It is the only sermon in his journal that is not in his own handwriting, and may have actually been an impromptu message. The journal indicates that it was copied by his wife, Catharine.[2] It is uncertain why she wrote it down rather than he, and whether she transcribed the sermon into the journal as he spoke or copied it from notes later. The neat, unrushed penmanship suggests the latter.

In *Sowing the Seed*, Shipley alludes to the parallels between his own science experiment with seeds and how the word of God is like a seed that has the capability to sprout within us, but is dependent on God to grow. Two of the people he mentions in this sermon—

George Harlan and Jenny Warder—were members of Cincinnati Monthly Meeting.[3] Harlan was the brother of the octogenarian Harriet Harlan Steer, who had counseled Shipley in his youth to "leave off some of the gayeties of [his] pleasures,"[4] and who was also concurrently serving as a minister of their meeting.[5] Warder was the 36-year-old daughter of John A. Warder, who had recently helped found the American Forestry Association.[6]

[Drawn to Christ][7]

And I, if I be lifted up from the earth, will draw all men unto me.
— JOHN 12:32

In Christ lifted up on the cross, we see love. In Christ lifted up at the right hand of the Father, we see power. Love to draw, power to uphold. It is love working in mighty power, and power working in mighty love.

Some years ago I attempted to go through the woods from one house to another. It was quite dark and as might have been expected, I soon went astray and worse, led my companion astray. But as I was struggling through the bushes, over the hindering logs, pulling myself and [my] friend out of the bogs, my eye caught sight of a light. I was sure it was in the house I wished to reach. I kept my eye fixed on that light, and it was but a short time until we reached our destination: soiled, scratched, but home.

There is a glass that is called Claude Lorraine. With this, the person looking into it sees what is behind them reproduced in detail of beauty. So would I lift up before you this past great act of our Lord that you may see for you Christ lifted up, as an act of the past so present before you that you shall be drawn to Him.

I visited a poor consumptive. He was washed and worn, and after some conversation, he was apparently reaching for some object beyond his grasp. I arose to assist him, when I saw he had what he wanted in his hand—a Testament. He kept it always with him—so let us keep Christ near us.

CHAPTER 1: PERSONAL ANECDOTES

You have known His drawing. We come to Christ:
> "Just as I am, poor, wretched, blind.
> Sight, riches, healing of the mind
> Yea, all I need, in Thee to find
> O Lamb of God, I come. I come."[8]

Why?

Because He is a *yearning*, tender, *sympathizing* friend.

Because help is laid on Him.

Because He gives rest. Come unto me, all ye that labor.[9]

Because in Him is *life*. Ye will not come to me, that ye might have life.[10]

Because in Him is redemption. In whom we have redemption through His blood.

Because in Him is welcome. Mercy. Healing.

[**Hidden Treasure**][11]

If ye then be risen with Christ, seek those things which are above, where Christ sitteth on the right hand of God. Set your affection (mind) on things above, not on things on the earth. For ye are dead, and your life is hid with Christ in God.
— COLOSSIANS 3:1-3

Is hid—literally, laid up in store.

"The whole growth of a lily . . . lies folded up within its bulb. Its leaves and blossoms are only a development, a revelation of what is in the root, only a manifestation of the fragrance and beauty—the spotless purity and attractive grace that are hidden within the apparently dry and unsightly scales of the root. And so Christ lies at the basis of, and involves the whole spiritual life. . . . All the individual life of the Christian, with its blossoms of holiness and its fruits of righteousness."[12]

"Just as there is provision made for the growth of the germ in the starchy contents of the seed, until it has attained an independent existence; so there is provision made in the nutritive tissue of the bulb . . . for the support of the plant which it produces. . . . The seed-principle of holiness had been lost out of human nature; the germ of eternal life had been withered in the soul by sin; but into the dry ground, that could bear naturally only thorns and briars for the burning, a new principle of life and holiness has been introduced from heaven, and now the aspect of the barren moral waste is changed. The life which man does not possess himself is got by a union of faith with Christ. The righteousness which man cannot work out by his own merits is stored up for him in Christ, who made an end of sin and brought in an everlasting righteousness. The fruits of the spirit . . . are yielded as products of grace when rooted . . . in Christ. . . . The Root is holy; be ye also holy."[13]

I remember last summer, when sailing, going up by a sunken vessel. Near it was anchored a small schooner, and from it a diver in submarine armor descended to the sunken ship. By the side of the vessel stood a man with a rubber hose in his hand. Through that hose the air was forced to the diver below. His source of life was hid in the air pumps that continually, steadily, uninterruptedly sent the air below. I [can] understand that it took a faith that came by teaching, by the witnessing of others, to enable that man to venture out of the air under the water wholly, entirely relying on another to give him a supply of air to breathe out of his natural element. I can appreciate his feelings as, tempted by the recompense of reward, he stepped for the first time into the wilderness and felt himself going down into death to find its newness of life.

Seek—set your minds as for hid treasures.

[Our Father's Mercy Seat][14]

At the Home for poor inebriates there was brought a woman of about forty years of age. I was much interested in her, and one morning on my way to school thought I would call on her. She was standing by the window fronting the street, and as I entered the room, beckoned for me to come near her. As I approached, she said, "Do you see that man who is overseeing the mixing of the mortar? That man is my husband, and I have not lived with him for fourteen years! Will you go and tell him that I am here?"

I saw before [me] a workman looking happy and comfortable in the faithful performance of his daily labor. Was it right to disturb his present life, which might be peaceful and quiet, with the revival of a great sorrow? God's word said, "What therefore God hath joined together, let not man put asunder."[15] The Lord would take care of [the] results.

I waited until the man returned to the house that he was repairing, and having obtained his name, asked of the employer if he had such a name on his list of workmen. He said he had, and would send him to me. A nearer view of his countenance discovered to me an open, honest expression of face, and as I thought of the errand on which I had come, and realized that my words must destroy his quiet of mind thus early in the day, my heart failed, and I felt almost as if I was about to run a knife into his heart.

I told him I supposed he had heard that the adjoining house was occupied by poor women who had become intemperate, and that some ladies had gone into the lower parts of the city to invite them to this Home that they might be rested and refreshed from their sad life and fitted for labor. That one of these women had told me that morning as she looked from the window that he was her husband!

In a moment his countenance altered. It was as if a cloud had cast its shadow over a green field which a few moments before was brightened by the sun's brightest rays. I waited in silence for strength to be given him. He looked up and said, "I suppose it is all true. When I married her, she was a respectable woman. *I* taught her to drink, but when I became a Christian, I promised the Lord that if I ever had the chance, I would help her as I had been helped. I will go now to see her."

I told him I would speak to the employer and see if it would be right for him to leave his work. He said he wished I would, and when he was asked, [the employer] very kindly consented at once.

On his entering the room, the look of recognition between them assured their beholders that they had once known a true fellowship of life. And when they both left, their faces bore evidence that with many tears had they met before our Father's mercy seat.

[Sowing the Seed][16]

My God shall supply all your need according to his riches in glory by Christ Jesus.   — PHILIPPIANS 4:19

I called this afternoon to see George Harlan who has been in the Cincinnati Hospital, [in] Room 8 [in the] private ward, for nearly two weeks on account of something like paralysis of the lower limbs. He told me he believed in the atonement of Christ and felt that his sins had been forgiven and related the following:

When engaged by the government in [the] Internal Revenue Department, the smallpox was raging in that part of the city where he was stationed. He had working with him a young man who had never been vaccinated. He warned him of the risk, and [the young man] often promised to be vaccinated. There occurring an afternoon when they were disengaged, [George] told him, "Now I will take you with me and you shall be vaccinated." At first he declined, then accepted the invitation. Then hesitated. But the invitation was again extended. "Come with me, it shall not cost you anything. I will take you to my own physician." But no—some other time. And in a week he was dead from smallpox.

There is sitting on my desk a glass partly filled with water. The water has been covered with cotton, and in turn a number of grains of wheat are scattered over the cotton. These have sent their rootlets into the water. The glass thus arranged was placed in a dark closet, and these put forth roots and plumule leaf. And [when] the wheat sprung up first in the dark, it was white, but now, having been brought in the light, it reflects the green color of light.

I was talking with Jenny Warder, and she spoke of the grain of wheat having the principle of "life in itself." Instantly my thought went to the "sowing of the seed."[17] And the seed is *the word*. And it is our duty to *sow the seed*. Its taking root and growing is dependent on other things.

The old theory of ministry among Friends was that the power should come to the hearer from the speaker, he "baptizing them in (into) the name of the Father, Son, and Holy Ghost."[18] As I now read the Bible, it is our duty to go forth and sow the seed as the Lord may direct us, but our dependence is on God who causes the seed sown "to grow up." It is not that we impart the Holy Ghost, but that to our hand is entrusted the sowing of the seed of truth. And the words I speak unto you are spirit and life.[19]

CHAPTER 2

Dramatic Narratives

If Shipley chose not to share much of his own personal religious experiences in his sermons, he nevertheless used considerable empathy and imagination to describe the thoughts and feelings of figures from Biblical times, both individuals actually mentioned in scripture and characters of his own contrivance.

Follow Me describes the call of Matthew. Here, Shipley not only provides the Biblical account of the disciple's background, but also speculates on what he had heard of Jesus's work and how he felt as he responded.

In *He Healed Them All*, Shipley describes not a specific individual, but rather the multitudes that went to be healed by Jesus. Nevertheless, Shipley personalizes them via the details he adds—a formerly blind mother gazing on the faces of her children, a formerly deaf grandfather listening to the loving words of his grandchildren and his old friends. In this way, Shipley encourages his listeners not only to relate to the humanity of the unnamed throngs, but to see Jesus through their eyes. Indeed, he goes even further, imagining Jesus's own feelings as he taught the crowd and observed their reactions.

In *My Father's Business*, Shipley focuses on the person of Jesus—not only on the man he was, but on what a man with his gifts could have been: wealthy, dignified, a worldly leader rather than the head of a band of socially unacceptable outsiders. Here Shipley imagines the thoughts of those with whom the young Jesus interacted, as well as his own parents. (The story of the young man who came to the city seeking his fortune, although told in the third person, could well be autobiographical.)

Atonement (which Murray once wrote in his journal as *at-one-ment*[1]) goes further back in time, and further in terms of Shipley's creative capabilities. Here he envisions the skepticism of an anonymous Jew as he watches Moses consecrate Aaron and his sons into the priesthood. In the story, the man's trust in Moses evolves into faith in the atonement provided by the animal sacrifice. This, of course, becomes an allegory for faith in the atoning sacrifice of Christ.

This Man Receiveth Sinners combines imaginative accounts of several New Testament stories—the prodigal son, the woman who anointed Jesus's feet with oil—with a likely apocryphal tale of a contemporary young woman's conversion experience. Shipley's journal attributes the story of the young woman to the English evangelist Geraldine Hooper. It was clearly not a description of a Quaker experience, since at the end the young woman takes communion—a practice Friends considered a spiritual rather than physical event that was not observed in their worship.

Lovest Thou Me. Feed My Sheep. Follow Me. reiterates a story about Thomas Hoopoo, a native Hawaiian and Christian convert who attended the Foreign Mission School operated by Presbyterians, Congregationalists, and other Protestants in Cornwall, Connecticut, in the early 1800s. The school included pupils from around the world, including some from the Indian subcontinent and Native American tribes, which might explain why Shipley described Hoopoo as attending a mission school "among the Indians." An account of the episode shared by Shipley appeared in *The Vermont Chronicle* in 1847, as well as other newspapers in New York, Boston, and elsewhere.[2] It is uncertain how Shipley became acquainted with the anecdote. A version of it was printed in a local Methodist journal, *Western Christian Advocate*, in 1850, but that version lacked some of the details that Shipley included in his telling.[3] Most of his narrative quotes phrases from the 1847 article verbatim. It is possible that the story had been retold often enough that it had become part of contemporaneous evangelical folklore.

Follow Me[4]

And as Jesus passed forth from thence, he saw a man, named Matthew, sitting at the receipt of custom: and he saith unto him, Follow me. And he arose, and followed Him.

— MATTHEW 9:9

This is Matthew's account of his own conversion. Levi was his old name. Levi was the servant of the law, and Matthew, God's free man. The other evangelists call him only Levi, which was his Hebrew name, but he always calls himself Matthew. Galilean by birth, a Jew by religion, and a publican by profession. His ordinary abode, Capernaum. It is probable he had a previous knowledge of the Lord's life and labors. Jesus had just healed the palsied man saying, "Arise and walk," after first saying, "Thy sins be forgiven thee." How long do you think that man was in having his sins forgiven? Instantaneously. This occurred in "his own city," Capernaum.[5]

And as Jesus passed from thence—"from thence," from performing this miracle and from having pronounced forgiveness, and "from thence" from his city, probably on the road near the sea of Tiberias—as he passed (or was passing), he passed the custom-house.

How very vividly must this scene have been before Matthew as he wrote it. He had probably heard of the leper that had been cleansed, of the centurion's servant in Capernaum that had been healed of palsy by *the word* of Jesus saying, "Go thy way; and as thou hast believed, so be [it] done unto thee."[6]

He had probably heard of Peter's mother-in-law being cured by *the touch* of Jesus. He had heard how at *the command* of Jesus the devils had been cast out. And Jesus had just not only done all these, but with utmost *tenderness* saying for the first time in his mission and with authority, "Thy sins be forgiven thee," and then silencing the caviling scribes, "But that ye may know [that] the Son of man hath power on earth to forgive sins," he said, "Arise, take up thy bed, and walk."[7]

And then [Jesus] went forth to the seaside, and all the multitude resorted unto him, *and he taught them*, and as he passed by he saw Levi. And in this fishing village, [Levi] must have heard of these wonderful works of Jesus, for the leper had blazed abroad his cure, for he had healed many that were sick of diverse diseases and cast out many devils. And now this man that cleansed the leper and the fever-stricken at his touch, that cast out devils and cured the palsied by his word, and that filled the boat with the miraculous draught of fishes, before him, ah! There was a heart that, publican and sinner as he was, was ready and attentive to Christ's word: Follow me.

Are there not those that have seen as great works among their friends? Those more leprous by sin have been cleansed by his word, devils have been cast out, palsied hands and feet have labored with their new-found strength. And now, oh sinner, thou has been sitting at the receipt of custom of this world, thou has known of these things, has not this same Jesus again and again said unto thee, Follow me? And thou has turned away from Him.

Do you think Matthew had nothing to give up and nothing to overcome? Do you think his part of gain had not had a warm place in his heart? Do you doubt there were the keen consequences of exaction and oppression resting on his conscience? Had he not all the strong legal prejudices of a Jew? Did he want to ask, "How?" He was a man of like passions with you. But Jesus was there, and he spoke to him. Their eyes met. There was a personal appeal. Follow me.

Persons say in certain circumstances many things pass through the brain in a moment. Follow me. It meant what Luke says, "He left all."[8] Yes, the choice was made. He had made a new choice in life. Have you made the choice? The Lord stands before you again this day and says, "Follow me." He means you and means you to leave all—*all*—and follow Him now. "Religion," said [a] young lady, "is the only thing I have been content to do by halves." You have not been content to love and please your mother in a half-hearted way. Matthew, as a Jew, left his legalism.

But what his first step in leaving all? Notice the next verse tells: "And Levi made him a great feast in his own house: and there was a great company of publicans and of others that sat down with them."[9] This was leaving all, in consecrating all. He left all. He left—his worldly ambitions, his not-allowed gains. He left his doubts and sense of unworthiness and weakness, and on the naked word of the

Lord, turned his back in hearty repentance on sins and unbelief, in full faith in the free grace of God, in full confidence in Him who has power on earth to forgive sin. He reckoned himself dead indeed unto sin—his own life—but alive unto God through Jesus Christ, and arose.

Arise, oh soul, today. Arise, turn thy face Christ-ward, and there shall come such a constraining sense of love that the very flow of love shall prompt what Matthew offered—his home, his means as an agency to draw his old associates to sit down and feast and be taught by the new leader he had learned to love. And he had learned that to leave all was to consecrate all. It was out of self, into Christ. "Entire surrender is the true source of power. It is not all to be saved *from*, it is something to be saved *to*."[10] From the custom-house and sin to following Jesus and holiness, for consecration is much more than resignation. But in the hearty consuming with the baptism of fire, as lime is burned out of the limestone, so does the soul find that [it] has heard the voice of Jesus saying "Follow me" and has arisen and followed Him.

We get all when we lose all.

This first step of Matthew was probably the characteristic of his life. The seeking to bring others to Christ to be taught by Him. Contrast Matthew and the other disciples at once following Christ, and the young man who had great possessions, to whom Christ [said], "[go] thy way, sell whatsoever thou hast, and give to the poor, and thou shalt have treasure in heaven: and come, take up the cross, and follow me. *And he was sad and went away grieved.*"[11] They were glad—he was sad. They followed—he went away. They were in joyful fellowship—he was grieved.

Contrast Peter in his first love, forsaking all—even the miraculous draught of fish—and following Him. And then when Jesus was arrested in the garden, he forsook him and fled, and Peter followed afar off.[12]

CHAPTER 2: DRAMATIC NARRATIVES

He Healed Them All[13]

And when they could not find by what way they might bring him in because of the multitude, they went upon the housetop, and let him down through the tiling with his couch into the midst before Jesus.[14] — LUKE 5:19

They came to Him, just as they were.[15] They exercised faith to come to Him and to touch Him on the statement of or sight of others that had been healed. Experience of healing only follows the faith of touch. Do you not suppose there were others in those towns who never came, and some who did not discern in the first incipient stage of disease that they were incurably affected? The whole multitude on their own felt [a] sense of need, and for their individual benefit to receive *sought* to touch Him. Each one as the example to the other. Not as the hand of a multitude, but the hands of multitudes of individuals. Individual needs. The sudden changes from hopeless sickness to sudden health, constantly going on as one after another touched and he healed them all. The sudden joy of many a parent or relative as their friends were healed.

[He] healed them *all*, all of a multitude, but it was a multitude that came to be healed. There was many a multitude of every town that never came. What became of all them that were healed, for at his death he was seen of 500 brethren, [yet] there were but 120 in the upper rooms.[16] In Luke 17, ten lepers were cleansed, and only one returns to give thanks. So multitudes have gone to God in time of extremity and have [been] relieved, but few returning to Him to give thanks.

What a strange scene. A group of friends drawing near a leper who had been an outcast. A wife and children embracing a clean father. A blind mother gazing on the faces of her children. A deaf, aged grandfather listening to the loving words of his grandchildren and his old friends. The breaking forth of dumb lips of some child, and groups of rejoicing friends, and still the multitudes (throng) sought to touch Jesus. And again, friends speak to their acquaintances and tell of this, that, and the other case. At his word those possessed with devils were quiet and restored, and he healed them *all*, and then he taught them.

How they must have listened to the strange new truths. The shouts, the rejoicings, the crowding to Jesus to thank him.

Blessed be ye poor, for yours is the kingdom of God.
Blessed are ye that hunger now, for ye shall be filled.
Blessed are ye that weep now, for ye shall laugh.
Blessed are ye when men shall hate you, etc. etc.[17]

He healed them and he taught them. You have come to him for earthly healing, and He gave it. In times of sorrow, misfortune, and need, and then he taught you. You came to him for healing, for the forgiveness of sin, and he healed you—and then he taught you.

What tender sympathy, what pitying love, what fellowship of joy and thanksgiving with the people. But how desiringly he watched their countenances to see what impressions his teachings made as he spake. To how many were his words there uttered on another occasion? "Ye seek me, not because ye saw the miracles, but because ye did eat of the loaves, and were filled."[18] How sad when he saw they were so full of their newfound blessing and forgot Him who blessed. When he says they gave Him their wonder, fear, gratitude, but not the love and faith of their hearts, became not his followers. He knew how to feel for the poor and the suffering, for he mingled with them as one in a common experience. How he must have felt afterwards. He was a man of sorrows and acquainted with grief. The people were astonished multitudes.[19]

It was because they were afflicted [that] they came to Jesus, and it was because they were afflicted that Jesus could use his power of healing to witness of His mission. It was because they were healed [that] they could tell what great things the Lord had done for them.

He has left us the example. The poor are always with us, the afflicted, the sorrowful, the despondent, those needing kneeling in its literal meaning, ministering, and we are to follow his steps. But it was not Christ's crowning labors that he healed a few sick folks, but [that] he preached the gospel and laid down his life, and we should preach his gospel—the glad tidings of a crucified and risen Redeemer—and lay down our lives.

What was it these people exercised when they came to Jesus to be healed? Answer: Faith. Many varied degrees of faith, some stronger than others, but in faith they desired one thing—to be cured—and Jesus always answers faith to grant the thing we stand in need of.

The hand reached out to heal and bless.

In life it was their bodies, but they were reached out [to] on the cross to heal the *festering wounds of sin*. "Then were there brought unto him little children, *that he should put his hands on them*, and pray: and the disciples rebuked them. But Jesus said, suffer little children, and forbid them not, to come unto me."[20]

The *hand* reached out. To heal on Earth. To bless. To atone on the cross. To endow with power from his throne.

What did anyone who thought of the outstretched hand that had blessed others think of *doing*? Nothing, but to go to it and to depend on what it would do.

The hand reached out. To intercede. To bestow gifts.

[In] Luke 8:43-48, the woman came behind and *touched* the hem of his garment, and immediately her issue of blood stanched, but the woman "came trembling, and falling down before him, *she declared unto him before all the people*" and he said, "Daughter, be of good comfort: thy faith hath made thee whole; go in peace."

Her faith in touching him healed her, but her testifying to him before all the people brought his *daughter [to] be of good comfort [and] go in peace*.

[My Father's Business][21]

And every man that striveth for the mastery is temperate in all things. Now they do it to obtain a corruptible crown; but we an incorruptible. I therefore so run, not as uncertainly; so fight I, not as one that beateth the air: but I keep under my body, and bring it into subjection.

— 1 CORINTHIANS 9:25-27

How patiently does the heir whose name from free grace has been written in the will of his benefactor wait for his inheritance? If wise, how does he both seek to please him who hath called him to be his heir and to fit himself for the station he has the promise in the will of receiving?

There are none of the epistles that should more fully challenge the attention of the officers of a church, its members, citizens, and especially the young, than the epistles to the Corinthians. Full of elucidations as regard the differences of gifts and their uses. Epistles noticeably directed to the encouragement of religious consecration and renunciation, and especially taking into consideration the influences upon all of a city devoted to learning, while it was the seat of pleasure and licentiousness. Here Paul had labored for a year and a half to build up a church. From time to time he hears of their dissensions and departures from the truth. Earnest efforts are made to overthrow his authority and influence. Grieved for their sins, he rebukes, warns, exhorts; but it is from a heart that considers not himself but Christ Jesus and their good.

The maxim of the world is live for the present; the Spirit's is live in the present for the future.

We have in the life of the Lord Jesus one so remarkable for steadfastness of purpose, so harmonious in its various stages, so opposite in its aim to the general intent of man, that we have need to seek some solution of the motive that induced such zeal, consecration, and self-renunciation.

His words of wisdom and keen insight into the characters of those about him, his ability to select the proper persons to carry out his intents, tell us of a man that might have amassed riches, or dignity, or been a leader in thought. At the age of twelve, taken by his parents to Jerusalem, he is found in the temple, sitting in the midst of the doctors, both *hearing* them and asking them questions. And all that heard him were astonished at his *understandings* and answers.

Did those doctors then resentfully listen to the wisdom of this child as they found themselves understood, as he heard their queries and propounded his questions to them, which in His childlike faith and grasping the spiritual truth even beyond their abilities, so that they were astonished? Or rather did they not mark him for a future scribe or lawyer, and words of praise so generally grateful to a lad were ready to be uttered, but were stilled by the quiet depth of wisdom of the boy?

His parents [were] awed by the company with whom they found him, involuntarily listening to his words of wisdom and seeing written on the faces of those whom they had never dared to approach the weight of the thoughts their boy's queries had suggested. For a moment they stand "amazed." But the parents' claims assert themselves, and seeing a mother's face, he turns to her. "Son," said Mary, "why hast thou thus dealt with us? Behold, thy father and I have sought thee sorrowing." Back comes the answer from his lips, solving for us the mystery of Christ's life, giving us the solution of the motive that induced him to seek not the results of the power of the body, mind, or spirit for himself, but "How is it that ye sought me? Wist ye not I must be about my Father's business?"[22]

He who would read aright the secrets of that wondrous life, which is left as an example that we may follow in his steps, must possess himself of this key to its secrets, this solution to its mysteries, and comprehend the depths of that Father's business, in the unfolding of the mystery in the hours that God was in Christ, reconciling the world unto himself, not imputing their trespasses unto them.

How few of us have had the direct thought before us of a goal in life that we desired to attain unto and have followed it with unwavering fidelity? I remember a countryman once who came to this city in his youth. Passing by the largest business house in our city, he said to himself, "I will be a partner in that house." With such an aim stimulated by right principles early inculcated, he grew up in integrity, temperance, and indomitable industry. Obtaining a situation in a similar branch of trade in a small way, he labored on, having one object in view, and attained it and a fortune. And he is now in our midst, one of our foremost active citizens, but his is a rare case.

From how many parents' heart comes the sigh, "Ah! My son is so easily influenced." Various winds have blown us hither and thither. The sneer, the laugh, or the approval of our young associates have blown us aside on our voyage of life. Drawn back by a parent's love, and by the good spirit of the Lord, only to yield to the winds of passion and our base desires. Brought to a stand, we feebly followed on, vacillating between various influences. The love of the world seizing us and pleasure's attraction being present before us, even the desires for success in this world could not resist the gusts of our desires. We wandered hither and thither, seeking to quaff the sweets of pleasures and draining the bitterness of the cup of sin.

Allured by the semblance of wisdom, we said, thought makes the man, and he who mostly truly thinks is most like Him who is truth. But drinking from a broken cistern into which only the surface water of the world had run, we drew not from the well of wisdom which God hath given us in the scriptures and marked not the wonderful words that fell from His mouth, "Thou sayest I am a King," nor the wonderful lesson written on His cross by Pilate, who knew not that he wrote but half the truth—Jesus of Nazareth, the King of the Jews. But now we know the King of the Gentiles also, and whose thought taking in only that which was ahead in his mind as to a King, including unto "for this cause came I into the world that I should bear witness unto the truth."[23]

Happy is that man or woman in whom God hath written with the finger of love a motto for life, and this the motto of Christ: *Wist ye not that I must be about my Father's business?*

[Atonement][24]

This is the thing which the Lord commanded to be done.
— LEVITICUS 8:5

As he hath done this day, so the Lord hath commanded to do, to make an atonement for you. — LEVITICUS 8:34

[For] today the Lord will appear unto you.
— LEVITICUS 9:4

And Moses said, This is the thing which the Lord commanded that ye should do: and the glory of the Lord shall appear unto you. — LEVITICUS 9:6

And Moses and Aaron went into the tabernacle of the congregation, and came out, and blessed the people: and the glory of the Lord appeared unto all the people. And there came a fire out from before the Lord, and consumed upon the altar the burnt offering and the fat: which when all the people saw, they shouted, and fell on their faces.

— LEVITICUS 9:23-24

The first seven chapters of Leviticus are occupied by instruction to Moses from the Lord as regards the offerings for the people. And when Moses gathered the assembly unto the door of the tabernacle of the congregation, his demand upon their faith was "This is the thing which the Lord commanded to be done." He then proceeds to consecrate Aaron and his sons to the priesthood, and you will find the directions in full in Exodus 28 and in Leviticus 8. You will find Moses doing "as the Lord commanded to be done." They are washed with water. The coat, the girdle, the robe, the ephod, the breast plate, the mitre, the holy crown, "as the Lord commanded Moses."

[With the] anointing oil, [Moses] anointed the tabernacle—the altar seven times, the altar and all the vessels. And he poured the anointing oil upon Aaron's head and anointed him to sanctify him. Aaron's sons [were] anointed "as the Lord commanded Moses." The sin offering, "as the Lord commanded Moses." The burnt offering, "as the Lord commanded Moses." The ram of consecration, "as the Lord commanded Moses." The oil and the blood sprinkled upon Aaron and his sons. The flesh and the bread to be eaten at the door of the tabernacle—the separation for seven days for consecration, "as he hath done this day, so the Lord hath commanded to do, to make an atonement for you."[25]

[In] Leviticus 9, Moses gives Aaron direction for offerings: for a sin offering and a burnt offering and a peace offering and a meat offering. "For today the Lord will appear unto you." Then follows Chapter 10, a warning against relying upon any form of righteousness without God's provision and with that which "he (the Lord) commanded . . . not."

The great central thought to which I have challenged your attention is the soul's reliance, acceptance, and blessing in the thing which the Lord commanded.

I can well understand the reasoning of the minds of many. God looks at the heart. He wants love to Him and love to my fellow man. Love to Him shown by obeying his commandments—living a life such as Christ lived, separate from sin, unselfish—and love to God shown in love to man. [Some might think,] "I can neither understand nor see what the crucifixion of Christ—other than an example to me of faithfulness to life's great principle—has to do with my sins. If I sin, I ask God to forgive it, and then I will try to do right in the future."

I bless God for an unshaken confidence in my own heart and in the heart of any man in the divine revelations of truths contained in the Scriptures. Here we find the answer to every doubt, here we find the knowledge of the things that pertain to our joy. Here, under the clean Light of the Holy Spirit, the eye of faith reads the provision for the uttermost need of the soul.

I can imagine a skeptical Jew watching the provision for the consecration of the priests, and he says, "Why, what use is that paraphernalia of gorgeous clothing, that golden plate, that golden crown? What benefit the death of that bullock, those rams? What nonsense and child's play to put a few drops of blood on the priests on their ear, their thumb, their toe. That sprinkling of blood upon everything—what a queer idea to mix oil with the blood and sprinkle over Aaron and his sons and their garments."

Yet there is one man in whose word he has complete trust, and that is Moses. He will never forget when he was a slave in Egypt, and the terrible plagues that Moses brought on the Egyptians. Nor the time when they were on the farther side of the Red Sea, and Pharaoh with his 600 chosen chariots and all the chariots of Egypt came in sight, pursuing after them, and he saw the pillar of cloud that had been before change and come between them and the Egyptians. Nor will he ever forget how Moses stretched forth his rod, and the water divided, and they went over in safety. Nor how that same Moses stood on the nearer bank after they had crossed, and reached forth his hand, and the Lord overthrew the Egyptians in the midst of the sea, and in the words of the Scripture, "And Israel saw that great work which the Lord did upon the Egyptians: and the people feared the Lord, and believed the Lord, and his servant Moses."[26]

Yes. He believed the Lord and he believed his servant Moses. But still, what is the use of these sacrifices and all this anointing? But Moses speaks, Moses whom he believes. He listens. "This is the thing which the Lord commanded to be done." Giving full faith to the messenger, he says, "Yes, it should be done."

He has an unintelligent faith: "I acknowledge—but why?" Again he sees Moses about to speak. With what an interest he listens. "This is the thing the Lord hath commanded to do, to make an atonement for you." Now faith has an intelligent reason: God whom he fears, reverences; His messenger, whose word he believes, carries out God's provision; and he knows God's ordered sacrifice atones.

But he is still [to] know more. He sees the high priest come forth, his high priest, whom his prophet set apart in the way God appointed, and speaks—blessed words to come from the high priest. He speaks to the children of Israel. It is no longer Moses doing for the high priest, but his own high priest that says to him as he stands one among the children of Israel. Take ye—the sin offering—the burnt offering—the peace offering—the meat offering—for today the Lord will appear unto you. Wonderful words.

There is to be made an atonement for him, and he is to see the Lord, but how? What a wonderful expectation fills his mind. Again, his prophet Moses speaks. "This is the thing which the Lord commanded ye should do." Do you suppose there is any more reasoning now? What is the use, do you suppose? Is he thinking about himself—his good actions—his repentance—his imitation of the life of benevolence? No. It is his atoning sacrifice, as the Lord commanded.

Bless the Lord. All his commands are promises, and all his promises, commands. Yes, at his command and his promise—when I see the blood, I will pass over you. Oh, he wants to see the blood! The knife falls, the blood flows, he sees his high priest sprinkle the blood upon the altar—*for me*—and this is the thing the Lord commanded to be done—to make *an atonement for me*. Wondrous love. Wondrous provision of love—*for me*. For a moment Moses and Aaron—prophet and high priest—pass from his gaze, into the tabernacle of the congregation—for a moment—and then lifting up their hands they blessed the people—and how he shall see the Lord is answered—for the glory of the Lord appeared unto all the people.

Ah, he will remember *the blood and the glory.*

I see them standing—[Jesus] led them forth as far as Bethany, and lifted up his hands, and it came to pass while he blessed them, he was parted from them, and carried up into heaven, and they worshipped him, and returned to Jerusalem with great joy.[27]

Oh thou who accepts God's words as true—hear now the wisdom and love of God. Christ died and yea rather is risen again.

Ever in the mind of that man, the memory of that moment will live, when first he saw the blood pour forth for the atonement of his sins, and the glory appeared. So look, so believe, so rejoice, so expect, for the glory of the Lord shall appear unto us. Christ died, yea rather is risen again, who *is* even at the right hand of God, who also maketh intercession for us.[28]

Who shall separate us from his love? [We are] more than conquerors. Nor any other creature shall be able to separate us from the love of God which is in Christ Jesus our Lord.

We read [in] Acts 7:55: "But he (Stephen), being full of the Holy Ghost, looked up steadfastly into heaven, and saw the glory of God, and Jesus standing on the right hand of God."

"Having therefore, brethren, boldness to enter into the holiest by the blood of Jesus."[29]

It is in the holiest we have seen the glory of the Lord. Washed in His blood, we entered the holiest. And in the presence of the Lord, the Spirit bore witness with our spirits, that we were the children of God and heirs.

It is our privilege not only to enter in, but to enter in to remain. There faith ripens to trust. There hope blooms into assurance. There thou art laboring and are heavy laden—find rest. In the presence of Christ and here is our abiding place. We live now, when we need not once and again to have an atoning sacrifice, but this hath He done once, so also may we ever walk in the Light as He is in the Light, rejoicing in His fellowship, and knowing the blood cleanseth.

This is our privilege—the blood cleansing—the Christian walking in Light—no need for the Christian ever to be separate from the blood, nor ever to be separate from the Light. There is no condemnation in Christ Jesus and no separation. Walking in the Light, clean under the blood, being filled with the Spirit.[30] Christ abides a victor over his conquered enemy. The blood. The blood, my friends. The glory of our risen King.

No, I am not slave, bought with a price. I am to glorify him with my body and my spirit, which are His. And will He who commands me to abide in Him be less faithful to abide in me? Let us go forward, victory written on our banners. The enemies of the Lord—for we fight not against flesh and blood, but against principalities and power, against the rulers of the darkness of this world—shall pale before us, and we shall more than conquer on through Him that loved us. He it is that will fight our battles for us.

This Man Receiveth Sinners[31]

Then drew near unto Him all the publicans and sinners for to hear him. And the Pharisees and scribes murmured, saying, This man receiveth sinners and eateth with them.

— LUKE 15:1-2

The scribes and Pharisees were there, but the publicans and sinners *drew near*, or were drawing near, and that to *hear* Him. The Pharisees were induced to listen, but the sinners drew near to hear Him. In Luke 11:29 it declares "when the people were gathered thick together" and Luke 12:1, "In the meantime (when He was in the house of the Pharisee who besought Him to dine with him, when [He] had pronounced woe against scribes and Pharisees, also lawyers), when there were gathered together an innumerable multitude of people, insomuch that they trode one upon another," He condescended to go into the houses of and teach the Pharisees.

In their traditional ritualistic spirit of thought, the Pharisees marveled Jesus had not washed before dinner. But now this thickly gathered innumerable company of publicans and sinners [were] drawing near unto Him, anxious to hear Him, to be taught, not with the lawyer-like sense of being teachers. "[The Pharisees began to urge him] vehemently, and to provoke him to speak of many things: laying wait for him, and seeking to catch something out of his mouth, *that they might accuse him.*"[32] But reading the hearts of these poor publicans and sinners as they drew *near* unto Him for to hear him *that they might be saved*, he caused them and the Pharisees to feel that He received them and ate with them.

How have you gathered this morning? Is it as a sinner? Is it to draw near unto Him? Is it for Him to receive you as a sinner and He as a Saviour? Is it to be fed by Him?

A lady young with a daily routine of novel-reading, morning calls, shopping, and dressing, and her evenings occupied with balls, soirees, theatres, and operas met with the loss of one who was very dear to her. To her young heart the trial was a crushing one. She mourned, murmured, and pined. Her own health became shattered and she went abroad. Weary, worn, and sad, she yearned for rest. She had lost a prize and in her heart was an aching void, which only the One she *knew not* could have filled. She determined to become religious; the world had ceased to woo her and its pleasures to charm her, and now nothing remained but to make herself a Christian, and this she tried her best to accomplish. The Bible was read night and morning; prayers were said. Yes, even delicate as she was, she would often rise at three o'clock in the morning and resort to the garden in the month of December, thinking that prayers said at such a cost would surely gain her admittance into heaven. Thus [she] passed six months and then returned hence, sad and chastened, with a yearning after something she possessed not: conversion.

One Sabbath evening she was led to go and hear an excellent minister. The minister gave as his text, "To die is gain." With zeal he portrayed those to whom to die would not be gain. After enumerating many classes he depicted the proud Pharisees, trusting to their own good works and righteousness, and then concluded by showing the character of them to whom to die would be gain.

She listened with rapt attention, tears—scalding tears—coursed down her cheeks. She had often wished to die, but now she felt that to her, proud Pharisee as she was, to die would not be gain. She returned to her home in agony of soul, etc. The week passed in misery and wretchedness: all her fancied righteousness had been torn in shreds. She could not read; she could not pray; and she knew not the simple plan of salvation.

Another Sabbath dawned and in the evening she attended the same church. The same minister proclaimed the gospel, this text was, "Lo! He cometh in clouds and every eye shall see Him." The arrow of conviction entered more deeply into her soul. If to die would not be gain, the Lord's coming would be worse still. How could she meet him? She returned home. The night of weeping was continuing, but ere long the morning of joy should break forth.

A friend remarked to her that if one were seen weeping so much in church, the people would think she was a great sinner. Her reply was prompt. "They will not think me a greater sinner than I think myself!" Another Sabbath and she started to the same church, remarking to a servant who accompanied her, "Unless I get some comfort tonight, I do not think I dare go again. It is too much for my mental frame." Entering the church she saw the communion table spread for the commemoration of the Lord's Supper. In her own breast she resolved she would not stay to it, the prayers she hardly heard. She craved some word which should afford her one gleam of light and hope.

With trembling eagerness, she listened for the text. It was announced, "This man receiveth sinners." O joyous news! Was it true? Then she might come. Was it true? Then she might be saved! Was it true? Then she would be received! She heard no more—she wanted nothing more. The burden was gone. The darkness was past. The void was filled. And peace such as the world giveth not hushed the troubled waters of her soul to rest. She did not turn away from the table of the Lord, for now *the blood* was applied to the lintel of her heart, she might eat the Lamb by faith.

Ah, my dear Friends, do you say, "To die would not be gain?" Do you shrink from giving account of the deeds done in the body? Has the Spirit shown you yourself as a sinner? Then hear the joyous word: "This man receiveth sinners."

It was the Pharisees that murmured saying, "This man receiveth sinners." They thought he should receive the ritualist, the moralist, the well-behaved classes, the attenders to religious duties, and they that thus conformed to His will He should receive. But blessed be His name, this man receiveth sinners.

He not only receives sinners, but permits himself to be received by them. "And when he saw Matthew sitting at the seat of custom, [he saith unto him], Follow me. It came to pass Jesus sat at meat in the house. Many publicans and sinners came and sat down with Him and His disciples. And when the Pharisees saw it, they said unto His disciples, Why eateth your master with publicans and sinners? But when Jesus heard that, he said unto them, They that be whole need not a physician, but they that are sick. But go ye and learn what that meaneth, I will have (love) mercy and not sacrifice: for I came not to call the righteous, but sinners to repentance."[33]

Who was this man that received sinners? He who has power on earth to forgive sins. He who so loved the world that He is the Lamb of God that taketh away [sins]. He who is our High Priest and Intercessor and has atoning blood to offer. He who ever lives to intercede for us. He who is our elder brother and feels we are laid upon him. He who sends the Spirit into us.

Come and let him press thee to His bosom; thy own unclean heart shall be washed by that blood that flows from his heart for thee.

He receiveth sinners. He does not merely give us a series of commandments and rules, as a governor or teacher, cold rules to be obeyed. No! Such were the teachings of the Pharisees! No! He received them. They felt they were welcome. As the frown of disapprobation settled down upon the face of the Pharisee as he saw the hated publican and vile sinner take a seat at the table, and in turn the sullen, resentful scowl spread over the face of the latter, I can see it change. The publican and sinner see the distinguished guest smile. His warm welcome to them, and they feel they have a friend who already receiveth them, and they forget the distinguished strangers for all eyes are fastened upon him. Oh, sinner, Jesus is here, and down the rows of their hearts his eye glances. Is any thinking, "I'll venture in. I know I am not worthy."? Oh, sinner, look at his face, read that tender, comforting, inviting, welcoming smile. Ah, yes! This man receiveth sinners.

CHAPTER 2: DRAMATIC NARRATIVES

In every heart, God has placed his white-winged message presager of good: hope. And we all look forward to that time when care and sorrows [are] over. The battle of life fought and the valley of the shadow of death passed, we shall be welcomed to an eternal inheritance, but it remains true. Oh, sinner! This man receiveth sinners. Not then—no, then He shall welcome *the blessed ones*. Come ye blessed of my Father—but now, He receiveth *sinners*. Yes, it is now! Then come *now*, now as a sinner, and be received and then eat with Him. Your heart at rest, peace made. He will break the bread and feed you, his guest—the prodigal received.

How did the father receive the sinner? He went to meet him—a great way off, fell on the neck of the sinner, kissed him, put on the ring and garment. Oh, yes, [Jesus] received sinners, but as a King. He welcomes, he names them son. He puts on the ring. He clothes them. Ah! He is the King and we are to be joint heirs with Christ. A royal reception!

Why was the Father so ready to receive the prodigal? Ah! He had waited a long time for him. He did not wait to put him on probation. No, heart asserted itself, round went his arms, burning tears of welcome were shed. And sinner, Christ has waited for you, and that is one of the meanings in the original of this word *receiveth*: has waited a long time, has seen you afar off, and now, oh, come.

A mother in Scotland, daughter a sinner in a distant city. Latch string always out. [The] daughter returned and found an open door, as it was.

There are plenty of Pharisees that will not receive you. There are plenty of sinners that will receive you, but what will they do? Only keep you in sin, drag you down to hell, add to its torments. Jesus receives to save, to lift you up to heaven. This man receiveth sinners and forgiveth sinners.

I see such a one. She comes where the master is a guest. No one receives her, no place at the table for her—no welcome from Simon the Pharisee. Shall she venture in? A look at Simon's face and her heart says, No! One look at the face of Jesus, and her feet have crossed the threshold. These feet that have trod the ways of sin and led so many others there. This woman which [was] a sinner, but lo! She stands at His feet. His feet soiled and hot with performing deeds of mercy and walking to teach the truth. She stands at His feet, burning tears course down her cheeks. She washes His feet with them. She wipes them with the long tresses of her hair. She kisses His feet. She pours forth her treasure—that alabaster box of ointment. It was intended perhaps for herself in her life of sin, but the ointment is poured upon His feet.

The Pharisee looks upon her and upon the Lord. A cold sneer is upon his face, and he spake within himself, "This man, if he were a prophet, would have known who and what manner of woman this is that toucheth him, for she is a sinner." Ah! How repulsive the touch of that broken-hearted sinner was to Simon; how dear it was to Christ. "Simon," it is the Lord [who] speaks. I can see the woman stop and listen. "Simon, I have somewhat to say unto thee." And he saith, "Master, say on." "There was a certain creditor which had two debtors. The one owed five hundred pence and the other fifty. And when they had nothing to pay, he frankly forgave them both. Tell me, therefore, which will love him most?" Simon answered and said, "I suppose that he to whom he forgave much." And He said unto him, "Thou hast rightly judged."[34]

Can you think how she listened? Five hundred pence. Yes, that was she—nothing to pay. Yes, that was she—forgave them both. What could it mean? But at that moment the red blood mounted to that brow, so seldom used to blush, for Jesus turned and said, "Simon, seest thou this woman? I entered into thy house and thou gavest me no water for my feet, but she has washed my feet with tears and wiped them with the hairs of her head. Thou gavest me no kiss, but this woman, since the time I came in, hath not ceased to kiss my feet. Mine head with oil thou did not anoint, but this woman hath anointed my feet with ointment. Wherefore I say unto thee, her sins, which are many, are forgiven, for *she loved much*, but to whom little is forgiven, the same loveth little."

Overcome with astonishment, with parted lips and waiting heart, she stands before Him, the image of surprised suspense. This time He speaks to her, His eyes meet her swimming eyes. "Thy sins are forgiven thee." And in answer to those who sat at meat with Him who began to say, "Who is this [who] forgiveth sins also?" He speaks: "Thy faith hath saved thee; go in peace." And this one went down to her house (her mother's perhaps, certainly not to her old life of sin), justified. Ah, yes, this man, this Jesus, the Lamb of God, this mediator, receiveth sinners, condemned sinners, guilty, sentenced sinners and says, "Thy sins are forgiven thee" and eateth with them. He is here—he is waiting for you to come to him. Do you come? For this man receiveth sinners and eateth with them.

Lovest Thou Me. Feed My Sheep. Follow Me.[35]

Jesus saith to Simon Peter, son of Jonas, lovest thou me more than these? He saith unto him, Yea, Lord; thou knowest that I love thee. He saith unto him, Feed my lambs. He saith to him again the second time, Simon, son of Jonas, lovest thou me? He saith unto him, Yea, Lord; thou knowest that I love thee. He saith unto him, Feed my sheep. He saith unto him a third time, Simon, son of Jonas, lovest thou me? Peter was grieved because he said unto him the third time, Lovest thou me? And he said unto him, Lord, thou knowest all things; thou knowest that I love thee. Jesus said unto him, Feed my sheep.
— JOHN 21:15-17

Peter was not grieved but pleased that Christ should reinstate him in His service—feed my sheep—but was grieved that his love was doubted. Feed my lambs. Keep my sheep. Feed (with suitable food) my sheep.

We are to be under-shepherds. The chief shepherd never forsakes (leaves) his flock. We work always under his eye. We shall have to give an account.

We are to love the sheep, our work, and the Master. We are to love the sheep, "for what shall a shepherd of the sheep do without love?"[36] But it is far more. It is for love to the Master we are to feed, keep, provide carefully.

If I were to ask, "How does the chief shepherd set us the example?" I hear your various answers. He will gather the lambs with his arm and carry them in his bosom. Again. He will lead them besides the still waters and in green pastures. Again. He calleth his own sheep by name and leadeth them out, saith one to whom the witness of the spirit is clear as to their being in the fold. A more timid, less trusting spirit says, "The voice of a stranger they will not follow." Another full of thanksgiving, "He is the good shepherd, the good shepherd layeth down his life for the flock."

Feed. Yes, daily. Unweariedly, when the lambs are willing to feed.

How this strikes at the root of that religious selfishness that says, "My piece of the loaf is so small, so little worth offering another that surely I have none to spare," instead of remembering that everyone is to break his piece and supply his neighbor.

And then see how "feed my sheep" is joined with "follow me" (verse 19). What God hath joined, let no man put asunder. But Peter followed him afar off.[37]

Thomas Hoopoo attended a mission school among the Indians. After some time he went with Deacon H. to New Brunswick to the house of the clergyman. On the evening of their arrival, a select company, including the clergyman, were invited to spend the evening with a celebrated attorney of the place. Thomas (then about sixteen years of age) accompanied them.

The lawyer entertained the company for a long time with asking Thomas about his native country, their customs, religion, enjoyments, etc., especially upon their religion compared with the Christian religion. At length the lawyer, who was not a religious man, ceased, and Thomas spoke out before them all.

"I am a poor heathen boy. It is not strange my blunders should amuse. But soon there will be a larger meeting than this. We shall all be there. They will ask us all one question: Do you love the Lord Jesus Christ? Now, sir, I think I can say, Yes. What will you say, sir?"

He ceased. A death-like stillness pervaded the hall. At length it was broken by a proposition from the lawyer that as the evening was far spent, they should have a season of devotion. Soon they separated and retired to their rooms, but there was no rest for the lawyer. The question of Thomas rang in his ear. "What will you say, sir?" He paced his room in anguish. The Spirit of God had touched his conscience. He found no rest till he could answer the thrilling question proposed by that "heathen boy" in the affirmative.

The Lord asked three questions that Peter answered.

"Whom say ye that I am?"

He saith unto Peter, "What, could ye not watch with me one hour"?

"Simon, son of Jonas, lovest thou me?"[38]

These questions are asked of each of us as to faith, obedience, love. In each of these interviews of Christ with his disciples as related by John, there is a central thought given.

Peace be unto you.[39]

Blessed are that have not seen and yet have believed.[40]

Lovest thou me.

CHAPTER 3

Parables, Allegories, and Analogies

In his own teaching, Jesus often used illustrative stories that his audience could easily relate to and remember. For early Quaker preachers, metaphors and allegories—particularly the contrast of light and dark—were an important tool to appeal to human emotions and express complex ideas.[1] Shipley leveraged similar techniques in some of his sermons, invoking both timeless imagery (such as comparing growing seeds to growing in faith) and more contemporary references to the technologies and events of his time.

In *Discovering the Ever-Present*, Shipley focuses on the marvels of relatively new technologies: telegraphy, electroplating, hydraulic power, steam engines, and photography. Yet the basis for them—electricity, water, and light—have always existed in the natural world. Shipley likens their discovery to the discovery of Christ, who according to the Gospel of John has likewise always existed.

After the turbulent Congressional election that occurred in Ohio on October 10, 1876,[2] the rights and responsibilities of citizenship were clearly on Shipley's mind. In *Rights of Heavenly Citizenship*, he compares being a citizen of an earthly nation to being a citizen of the heavenly kingdom. He also asserts that becoming a "naturalized" citizen of the heavenly kingdom through justification is not sufficient; obeying the will and direction of the enemy (implicitly, worldly or evil influences) rather than God would cause the citizen to "suffer the traitor's doom, and his right of citizenship will not save him." At the end of this sermon, Shipley reiterates a very Quakerly metaphor, equating the light that God created when forming the world with the Light of Jesus coming into the world. Shipley's journal indicates that this sermon was given on a Saturday at 7:30 PM, and the use of *we* in the introductory paragraph suggests that this message might have been part of a series of sermons given by various ministers, perhaps at evening revival meetings.

CHAPTER 3: PARABLES, ALLEGORIES, AND ANALOGIES

The message *Expecting and Realizing* was delivered at a mission meeting in Kendal, England, apparently part of a series of public events for people of diverse backgrounds. Shipley uses the example of cultivating produce on borrowed land to distinguish those who outwardly demonstrate virtues from those for whom the outward virtues are the result of an inward conversion.

This sermon also tells a story of a man who realized that his health was endangered, and that he could recover only when he both changed his habits and took his medicine. The recognition of physical threat is analogous to the awareness of spiritual peril; changing his habits reflects turning away from sin, and taking his medicine is allowing God to cure his soul.

Lastly, Shipley retells Jesus's parable of sowing the seeds, but with a twist. In Shipley's version, the soil is an active participant in the tale rather than just a passive entity. At first the soil resists the efforts of the gardener, then blames the gardener for not making itself immediately productive, and finally trusts that the gardener knows what he is doing, that in the seed is life, and that the conditions would ultimately be right for the seed to grow.

Expecting and Realizing is also Shipley's most explicit message about the necessity and nature of conversion. Apart from a passing reference in *No Difference*, it is the only sermon where he uses the phrase *born again*, which he considers a spiritual experience that occurs at some point in life following physical birth. Shipley sees God, Christ, and the individual playing three separate but simultaneous roles in the process. God's role is making the individual's heart open to the truth of its sinful state and entire dependence on God. Christ's role, through his death and resurrection, makes the forgiveness of sin possible. The individual's role is to repent, to recognize the saving work of Jesus, and to believe that as a result God will produce good works in one's life.

In *Yield*, Shipley presents multiple allegories for submitting to the will of God, such as a child allowing his hand to be controlled as he is taught to write, or an army being responsive to the orders of its commander.

In *Grace*, Shipley compares the weighing of gold pieces in the Bank of England to the final judgment awaiting those who come up short. He likewise describes being within national boundaries as being within the boundaries of sin.

Shipley himself had poor vision,[3] so he had first-hand experience with the allegory in *Invisible*. He describes how a nearsighted man becomes more aware of the beauty around him when he gets more powerful lenses for his glasses. The beauty was always there; he just needed it to be revealed to him. Shipley quickly segues from this positive image, however, to harshly criticize Quakers who believe that their practice of silent worship in and of itself constitutes being spiritually minded. Silence can disguise an empty mind, or an earthly one. What good, he asks, are the best lenses to a man whose eyesight is impaired by the cataract of unbelief?

Although *Direct* demonstrates several of Shipley's rhetorical techniques, its ultimate theme is the analogy between trusting the gondolier to navigate the canals of Venice and trusting God to direct our paths in life.

[Discovering the Ever-Present][4]

Have I been so long time with you, and yet hast thou not known me, Philip? — JOHN 14:9

The discoveries of the present day are continually saying to us of the gifts of God what He who is the gift of God thus speaks of himself. Man is astonished that he should so long have been ignorant of electricity, with all its benefits of telegraphy [and] electroplating, and of the forces of water, as it now yields itself his willing servant in its hydraulic powers, or changed into steam becomes his mighty instrument in all the various applications [where] we now use it. These and the powers of light applied to photography and numerous other discoveries all utter to our lower natures the same testimony, "Have I been so long time with you and yet hast thou not known me?"

There are more here today to whom these words are the expressions of their present experience. Having listened to the gospel expounded, read and talked of Christ as the Savior, they today wonder that Christ should have been so long time with them and yet they should not have known Him. Can we explain this apprehension of the truth? Can we give any reason to ourselves why "This is a faithful saying . . . that Christ Jesus came into the world to save sinners"[5] should be to us this morning a message of perfect peace, when we have listened to it so often without it being other than a truism which we do not deny? Yes. It is that the Holy Spirit has visited our hearts and shown us that we were sinners and needed *just such a Savior.*

Rights of Heavenly Citizenship[6]

That at that time ye were without Christ, being aliens from the commonwealth of Israel, and strangers from the covenants of promise, having no hope, and without God in the world: But now in Christ Jesus ye who sometimes were far off are made right by the blood of Christ. For he is our peace, who hath made both one, and hath broken down the middle wall of partition between us; having abolished in his flesh the enmity, even the law of commandments contained in ordinances; for to make in himself of twain one new man, so making peace; and that he might reconcile both unto God in one body by the cross, having slain the enmity thereby: and came and preached peace to you which were afar off, and to them that were nigh. For through him we both have access by one Spirit unto the Father. Now therefore ye are no more strangers and foreigners, but fellow citizens with the saints, and of the household of God.

— EPHESIANS 2:12-19

Daily have we set before you expositions of God's love to man in the gift of His son. God's substitution of the just and the pure for the unjust and those stained with sin. By every process of reasoning, of every appeal to your own felt need, by the testimony of those who have proved for themselves Christ to be their burden-bearer, we have appealed to you to recognize, heed, believe, and trust in Jesus Christ as the great substitute for you.

For—in the place of—you. Words cannot be too plain, figures too simple, application too pointed to effect the end of an open ear to the word of divine revelation. "The Lord hath laid on him the iniquity of us all."[7]

There is another truth equally important. Not simply naturalization of a foreigner by free grace from the act of another, but the maintenance of that new loyalty. For naturalization is not of works, but of grace. It is conferred upon him who wills to receive it. A man may live in another country, be a law-obedient resident, reap many advantages accruing to a resident, and yet unless he renounce his old allegiance and accept the new, he has not a single right of citizenship. There must be renunciation and consecration. There must be faith and acceptance of free grace, or he will never be a citizen.

There may be the clearest comprehension of the laws of citizenship. He may be able to lecture upon them with the ability of a Blackstone or a Story.[8] He may be convinced of the advantages that accrue from citizenship, yet his clearness of knowledge and simplicity of exposition will never make him a citizen.

Again, he may have been naturalized, he may have exercised every right of citizenship, he may have commanded the armies of his adopted country, yet if he be dallying with the enemy, if he be betraying the trusts reposed in him, if he be yielding up his obedience to the will and direction of the enemy, he needs but to be discovered, and he will be tried and suffer the traitor's doom, and his right of citizenship will not save him. Rather it will prove the argument for justice and not mercy, for retribution as in the violator of grace.

There is a citizenship to be acquired, but there is a citizenship to be maintained. The recent election, as it has appealed to our necessities, has caused many a man to speed across the country to cast his ballot on that side of the question that seemed to him the standard of justice, probity, and national health. How much more is this true concerning our citizenship which is in heaven?

Now which of these questions are you considering, and is it the one which at present is the all-important one to you? Are you a citizen? If not, your rights are those of aliens, not of citizens. When you are traveling in a strange country, you want to know who your Consul is and what claims you have for him to undertake for you. But your right of citizenship [is] in another country.

The Lord Jesus tells us of only one way to become citizens of another country, even a heavenly [one], and it is to be born citizens. "With a great sum obtained I this freedom," said the centurion to Paul, but [Paul replied], "I was free born."[9]

New creatures, old things passed away. The new birth is an act of creation and can only come from God. We are entirely dependent on Him, not by might nor by power, but by spirit. The Spirit moved upon the face of the waters, when all was without form and void, and God said, "Let there be light."[10] I am come a light into the world, where sin abounded.[11]

[Expecting and Realizing][12]

My dear friends, I want to say a few words about expecting and realizing. These are the subjects about which I have spoken the past two evenings. Expect to be converted. Realize you are converted. Now let us review our lessons.

The impenitent thief asked—prayed, if you please—of the Lord to save him from the cross, but he did not expect even that. The penitent thief said, "We suffer justly . . . Lord, remember me when thou comest into thy kingdom."[13] He expected what he asked, and he realized what he expected and more, too, but he could only realize it by believing Christ's words.

What do you expect conversion to be? Quitting drinking, swearing, lying, Sabbath breaking, evil speaking, tattling, laziness, anger, vanity, pride? Commencing to be sober, speak the truth and pure words, church going, kindness to others, industry, gentleness, simplicity, unselfishness, humility? Yes? No?

If I had here some pine cones, acorns, chestnuts, walnuts, peaches, apples, oranges, grass wheat, oats, turnips, carrots, and I said to you, "Look at my beautiful forests, see my tall pine trees, my majestic oak, my green chestnut tree, my spreading walnut trees"— if I said, "Look here at my orchards, my peach, apple, and orange trees"—if I pointed to the grass wheat, oats, turnips, and carrots and said, "Look at my farms, there is my pasture, here is my wheat field and next to [it] my field of oats, just over there are my two fields of turnips and carrots"—you would say to me, "Friend, these are the products of such forests, trees, and fields, but you may have all these fruits and yet own none of the fields. Perhaps you have only bought or borrowed them."

And that is pretty much the fact with many people who have quit or seemed to quit the worst sins, and seem to have some of the virtues. They have either bought or borrowed the virtues—bought them with hard exertions to overcome their temptations, or borrowed them by trying to wear the fruits of the tree of life. No, I tell [you], to be converted is not simply having the fruits of a good life, and it never is without having them.

A man may quit all the sins of the first class and have a life embracing most all of the [virtues], and have a heart as hard as a stone towards God. What then are we [to] expect [when we are] converted? Let me say now so that you will not misunderstand. If you are converted, you will increasingly show the opposite virtues to your former sins. If you are converted all the way through, if you have been stingy, you will become generous. If you have been idle, you will become industrious. And if you have been an ugly, cross man, woman, or child, you will become loving and kind.

What is it to be converted? What do you expect? That you will *feel* terribly the sinfulness of your sins? That you will *feel* exceeding sorrowful, and your heart pierced with anguish? That you will *feel* the same experiences that others have had? Or that with a hearty turning away from the known sinfulness of your lives and from your own efforts to be good and looking up unto Jesus crucified for you, you cannot be converted without also *feeling* great joy, great peace, just as others have said they felt?

Far be it from me to encourage any man to think he can voluntarily go on in his sins and hope he is a converted man. Far be it from me to make you less watchful to live in all that a Christian should. Far be it from me to lessen the consciousness of your own sinfulness or to take away from the joy of your peace. But I want

CHAPTER 3: PARABLES, ALLEGORIES, AND ANALOGIES

you to expect (to look for conversion itself) and to realize (to know Jesus as your Savior).

Conversion is to be born again. That which is born of the flesh is flesh, but that which is born of the Spirit is spirit. To be born again is then something that God does.

I am a new man, says a friend [of ours] who left us broken down in health, perhaps from his own bad life, and who went away to die. How did it happen, [we ask], how did you become a new man? Oh, I quit my old habits that were ruining my health, and I adopted good habits. Well, did that make a new man of you? Oh, no, that only gave the medicine the chance to work. It was the medicine then that took hold of your disease? Yes, but it would have been no use for me to use it and keep up my old evil life. Well, what made you quit your old life all at once and take that medicine? Because I became convinced if I continued as I was, I should die, and if I did not use the means to recover, I should die also.

Here is conviction, repentance, and conversion. Christ taught Nicodemus what was necessary for man. First, he must be born again (born from above). That is *God's* work. Second, as Moses lifted up [the serpent in the wilderness], so must the Son of Man be lifted up. *Christ's* work. Third, that whosoever believeth in Him—*man's* work. And all this is going forward at the same time in the heart that God has tendered under the truth.[14]

The earth cannot bring forth from itself life-producing and life-giving grain and fruit. What the scripture says is true; the ground is cursed. Nor can man produce the Spirit or His fruits; that which is born of flesh is flesh. And the first step is the entire convincement of inability to do God's work. We must be born again, and only God can do it. This should bring the soul to the footstool of prayer. And the moment the soul thus realizes the need of another hand—and that the hand of God—and looks to that hand, they are not far from the kingdom of heaven.

At once rises the next lesson Christ teaches. "Even so must the Son of Man be lifted up."[15] And He has been. Oh! What a necessity! For God so loved the world, that He gave His only begotten Son.[16] Nothing else, since God selected that was to be the means of convincing men not only of their sins against God, but their sin against God—their false thoughts of God. The law said, You have sinned, and the soul that sinneth shall surely die.[17] And your hearts said, God knows my sins and He condemns [me]. But He gave His only begotten Son that, knowing our sins, He might forgive them. God *has* visited our hearts that we might be born again. Christ *has* been lifted up, and *has* born our sins in his own body on the tree. *What remains? That we believe.*

Is God to you your judge, or is Christ your Friend? Let me put before you a piece of stony ground.[18] Suppose it can think, speak, and act. The gardener comes to it and scatters some seed on it. The fowls gather some and the rest dries up. He comes [back], there is nothing. He says to the rocky ground, "See, I have proved you cannot produce anything." And the rocky ground says, "I am content, I don't care to produce." And yet the rocky ground knows that the neighboring forest with its beautiful trees or its adjoining fields rich in grain, in fruit, and in flowers are the attractive ones that the gardener who owns all is pleased with, and which are accomplishing some good.

Again the gardener comes, and half sulkily the stony ground yields itself to the visitations of the gardener, and its stony bases are overturned and thrown up onto heaps. And the gardener sows some seeds, and when he is gone, the ground says, "If he wanted me to be a field, why did he not make me like that turnip field over there with splendid fine turnips growing in [it], all green and beautiful, long white turnips at the bottom? As for these miserable little dry seeds, I don't believe they are any account. I won't have them." And out it throws them. Oh foolish field!

Oh foolish hearts, upon whom the gardener has been turning his hands and bringing conviction to thy heart and sowing some true seeds of repentance and faith—believe! Believe what? Why, that thou art no longer the barren stony ground, but a field the Master has selected for his own, and that He who has begun a good work will carry it forward. He will build a wall about thee with the stones gathered from off thee. He will enrich thy soil with the gifts of his love and grace, and make the good ground, and sowing in thee such seed as He knows thou art able to bring forth, shall yet make thee one in beauty with the fields whom he redeemed not at the eleventh hour.

And now what did the field feel if it was changed in thought? It felt the seed in itself, the dry seed, but it believed the gardener knew what life there was in the seed. It believed that dew, rain, and sunshine would not be wanting, that while it might not understand, it was the gardener that did. It would expect to be a fruitful field in yielding itself to the gardener's care, and in good time it would realize it. It would say, "There is that heap of stones, that shows he cares." It is true they are outside, but the seed could not grow if they were inside. No more can God's seed of grace. And sins and that work of all sin, the sin of unbelief—out with it, away the stones. It is a rock; you cannot get it out. Do you want to be rid of it? *Tell the Master.*

Yield[19]

Neither yield ye your members as instruments of unrighteousness unto sin: but yield yourselves unto God, as those that are alive from the dead, and your members as instruments of righteousness unto God. — ROMANS 6:13

Circumcise therefore the foreskin of your heart, and be no more stiff-necked. — DEUTERONOMY 10:16

And the Lord thy God will circumcise thine heart, and the heart of thy seed, to love the Lord thy God with all thine heart, and with all thy soul, that thou mayest live.
— DEUTERONOMY 30:6

The devil was as much the devil when he changed himself into an angel of light.[20] And stiff-neckedness or strong will, our stiffness of will, is much the same when we hold our opinions with *undue* firmness, even in religious matters. Let our *wills be supple.* When you have a child's hand in yours to guide it to write, when he relaxes his control over it and surrenders it to you, *your handwriting* can be discerned though *another's hand holds the pen.* Oh, for suppleness of heart and will! Supple meaning pliable, flexible.

This quality does not imply want of decision, fixedness of purpose, and power. But as an army has all these, yet is perfectly pliable and instantly responsive to the will of its commander, so is it also one in that will as soon as conscious of it.

It involves accepting the whole truth by faith. Forgiveness of sin. In putting away unbelief and standing in Christ by faith. Yielding ourselves as those that are alive from the dead.

Now be ye not stiff-necked (harden not your necks) as your fathers were, but yield yourselves (give the hand) unto the Lord.[21]

You have been in a mill where there is a great deal of machinery, when imperfect work is produced where sometimes good work is finished. The owner does not cast aside the machinery; he looks for the cause, oils it, corrects the cause, and does it *at once*.

I have seen a great grindstone which was quite capable to do good work riven into three pieces because it was caused to revolve to the extreme of safety, and it proved to be beyond it.[22]

The word *present*—"I beseech you therefore, brethren, by the mercies of God, that ye present your bodies"[23]—is the same translated *yield*.[24]

To present: παραστῆσαι. The expression which was used [for] placing the sacrificial beast before the altar conveys the thought of the *complete resignation and readiness* which on the one hand does not in the least hesitate, but on the other makes no intrusion by an arbitrary slaying [of] the offering.

It is the altar that sanctifies.

Grace[25]

For there is no difference: for all have sinned, and come short of the glory of God; being justified freely by his grace through the redemption that is in Christ Jesus. — ROMANS 3:22-24

I visited the room in The Bank of England where the gold is tried by weighing—that is, brought into this government agency. A delicate machine is so arranged as to carry steadily forward to the scales piece after piece to be weighed; the forward motion is very slow but

CHAPTER 3: PARABLES, ALLEGORIES, AND ANALOGIES

very certain. The time of trial is approaching, and as you watch, the row of gold coin pieces gradually advancing, the thought [comes] of the final judgment when it shall be said, "He that is unjust, let him be unjust still: and he which is filthy, let him be filthy still: and he that is righteous, let him be righteous still: and he that is holy, let him be holy still. And behold, I come quickly; and my reward is with me, to give every man according as his work shall be."[26]

Gradually as the piece approached the scale, you saw the moment had arrived. Another moment it was weighed, and the least single gram of deficiency from the standard determined the matter as well as for those that were many grams deficient. They were all equally cast out on the *left* hand, while those of standard weight passed to the *right*. For there was no difference—they came short.

He shall say to those on the left, *"Depart from me,"* and to those on the right, *"Come, inherit."*[27]

For there is no difference. A man is just as much in the United States when he is in New York as when he reaches the center of the continent. In former days, the slave who fled from the United States, when he landed in Canada, was as free as when he crossed to England. And while we are all ready to cry out against the large crimes so prevalent, let us remember "he that is unjust in the least is unjust also in much."[28] There is no difference. [Jesus] speaks to the man that is only an inch within the forbidden territory. The soul that sinneth, it shall die. For all have *sinned* and *come short* of the glory of God. There is no difference.

As we read Romans 3 to the twenty-fifth verse, and read the black catalogue of sins and the blackness of sin, [the Apostle Paul] is looking upon the earth in the shadow of the darkness of transgression and evil. Is there not some bright earth flame to take away from the terror? None. For all have sinned. But behold, there rises a star in the east, and it guides us to Bethlehem. And John's voice cries, "Repent! Behold the Lamb of God!"[29] And Christ says, "Come. I am come a light into the world, that ye may not walk in darkness but may be the light of life."[30]

In a recent decision in our city, in a case where a number of merchants combined together to control a particular class of merchandise, [Judge Emmons said] "The partition between the scope and operations of this organization and actual crime is so thin as to be hardly worth discussing," so the *Cincinnati Gazette* reports it.[31]

And while the gigantic frauds against the government in various places—this habit of forming [syndicates] to control the gold of the country, articles of merchandise[32]—has thus been [labeled] as so nearly approaching crime as hardly to be worth discussing, it behooves everyone to ask ourselves whether there be not customs and practices in our business, habits, actions, [or] thoughts that need only the Light of the gospel for us, as we see them in God's Light and see the motive that prompted them, to exclaim, "There is no difference."

Invisible[33]

Now unto the King eternal, immortal, invisible, the only wise God, be honour and glory for ever and ever. Amen.
— 1 TIMOTHY 1:17

But the hour cometh, and now is, when the true worshippers shall worship the Father in spirit and in truth: for the Father seeketh such to worship him. God is a Spirit: and they that worship him must worship him in spirit and in truth.
— JOHN 4:23-24

For we know that the law is spiritual. — ROMANS 7:14

Carnal: flesh-like. Spiritual: spirit-like. The more our spiritual nature is developed, the more our religious perceptions are keenly alive to observe not the outward action, but the inward spring of action.

An increase of spirituality is like a man who is nearsighted. He for the first time is given a pair of concave glasses of weak power. Instantly, an unknown world *that has been about him all his life* comes to his view. Flowers bloom on every side. The beauty of the foliage entrances his eye. Again, a higher power is given to him. New life appears, delicate forms of beauty in the flowers he has just found charm his mind. The exquisite variety of forms in nature fills his mind with thoughts of the versatility of divine power, but again he changes to a focus in the glass that gives his eye its just power. And now, the world again becomes new to him. His perceptions are awakened by the medium that permits his naturally imperfect powers to discern what was formed for perfect sight. So is the natural man. The undimmed spirit alone reveals God and His works.

We speak of being spiritually minded in worship [because we do] not believe in the Pope as the Catholics, or have a liturgy like the Episcopalians, or observe the ordinances commonly observed by other denominations, or [have] systematically arranged forms of worship as most religious bodies do. [We presume] we are spiritually observing worship, as if this negation of outward surroundings would, in our quietness and form of silence, be spiritual worship.

An empty mind, and silence. A mind full of earthly sins, passions, fears, doubts, and unbelief, and silence. And either state, with all the surroundings of ministry or silence, is not worship, nor spiritual mindedness. Carnal mindedness is a mind flesh-like, and spiritual mindedness is a mind spirit-like.

Is thy heart thus today, or has the ploughshare of conviction been making way for the seed of living faith? Is the hand of the Lord seeking to take the white lilies of thy natural gifts and graces of character, and from his pierced hand imparting the royal mark of his redeeming love?

But what avails the most perfect glasses to a man born blind? What advantages the most perfect lens to the man over whose eyes has come the cataract of unbelief or the beam of anger, resentments, and unbridled passion?

Bengel quotes Ephraim Syrus: "The apostle called men, who lived according to nature, *natural*, ψυχικούς; those who live contrary to nature, *carnal*, σαρκικούς; but those are *spiritual*, πνευματικοὶ, who even change their nature into the spirit."[34]

Spiritual mindedness flourishes only on one wayside—and that is the straight and narrow way—and grows in no garden save where the Master is the gardener. The pathway of obedience ever is the footpath of the straight and narrow way, and only in its wayside do the fruits of spirituality grow to perfection.

Leighton says, "Certainly . . . the most frequent and skillful speaking of the word, severed from the growth here mentioned, misses the true end of the word. If any one's head or tongue should grow apace, and all the rest stand at a stay, it would certainly make him a monster. . . . He that is still learning to be more in Jesus Christ, and less in himself, to have all his dependence and comfort in him, is doubtless a growing believer."[35]

It is not contact with "the philosopher's stone," so long sought, that is to turn all things into gold, but it is contact with the rock, Christ Jesus, that shall change all the mean and ordinary actions of life into the golden offerings of praise.

Leighton says, "Men aiming at self-righteousness by the law, and desirous of that *as cheap as might be*, with *the least pains*, not being willing or able to rise to its perfection, drew it down and shaped it to their imperfection: cut it to the measure of external obedience, and that of the easiest size."[36]

Kempis [writes,] "He that has known the power of the spiritual life, and withdrawn his attention from the perishing interests of the world, is not dependent on time or place for the exercise of devotion. He can soon recollect himself, because he is never wholly engaged by sensible objects. . . . Constant experience has convinced him, that the soul is no further obstructed and disturbed in its progress towards perfection, than as it is under the power and influence of the present life."[37]

Let us inquire. Do we know a person who is a believer in Jesus Christ, but whose trust is in the outward forms of religion—the morning and evening prayer, family worship, church services, ordinances, prayer meetings, etc.? Who bridles not his tongue, and spares the best of his flock, and seeks to give a mite and calls it the widow's mite when she gave all, and he gives only what will look respectable? Is that spiritual religion? No matter even if he be one who, on the other hand, sits in silence instead of kneeling in prayer, denies himself the elegances of life, dispenses in worship with all forms, and gives liberally in charities, but whose heart has never melted under the news of the glad tidings of the gospel so as to say, Christ is mine? And to know what spirituality means in saying, I am

Christ's? For me, to live is Christ. In fact, to be able to say, "I have the mind of Christ" and to know not only what it is to deny himself, but to follow Him—thus *giving himself*.[38]

Direct[39]

Oh Lord, I know that the way of man is not in himself: it is not in man that walketh to direct his steps.
— JEREMIAH 10:23

Joseph, the ruler of all Egypt, wept aloud and said unto his brethren, "I am Joseph your brother, whom ye sold into Egypt. Now therefore be not grieved, nor angry with yourselves, that ye sold me hither: for God did send me before you to preserve life. . . . So now it was not you that sent me hither, but God."[40] Such a man could say, "Oh Lord, *I know* that the way of man is not in himself."

Our Lord stands before Pilate, silent, and gave him no answers. Pilate said, "Knoweth thou not that I have power to crucify thee, and have power to release thee?" Jesus answered, "Thou couldst have no power at all against me, except it were given thee from above."[41]

The High Priest Caiaphas said, "Ye know nothing at all, nor consider that is expedient for us, that one man should die for the people, and that the whole nation perish not."[42]

O Lord, I know that the way of man is not in himself. Charles IX gave the orders for the bells to ring out the massacre of death of Protestants on Bartholomew's Day 1572. He expired bathed in his own blood, which burst from his veins whilst he exclaimed, "What bloodshed, what murders! I know not where I am. How will all this end? What shall I do? I am lost forever. I know it."[43]

What a terrible *know* that is. It is not in man to direct his steps. And he may know that the steps of a good man are ordered by the Lord.[44]

Take the life of David. The Lord said [to Samuel], "Go, I will send thee to Jesse the Bethlehemite: for I have provided me a king among his sons." [Samuel] looks on Eliab and says, "Surely the anointed of the Lord is before him." But the Lord said, "The Lord seeth not as man seeth." And Samuel said, "The Lord hath not chosen these." The youngest came. The Lord said, "Arise, anoint him: for this is he." And the very qualifications God has given him is the Lord's providential means to bring him near the king and before the people. Saul's troubled spirit and David's gift: cunning in playing, and a mighty valiant man, and a man of war, and prudent in matters, and a comely person and the Lord is with him."[45]

Goliath and David's victory. Saul's anger and Jonathan's friendship. Saul's pursuit of David and David's experience of faith in God's deliverance and in answered prayer. All fit this anointed one for the place of king, and in his psalms, he still says to those who are wearied with the struggle with life, with sin and sorrow, "Now know I that the Lord saveth his anointed; he will hear him from his holy heaven with the saving strength of his right hand."[46] And Jeremiah re-echoes, "I know that the way of man is not in himself."

Dear friends, have we this knowledge as a controlling faith in our hearts, so that in the ordering and disposing [of] our lives, our query is, what is Thy will concerning us?

In Venice you watch the gondolier as he stands with his long, crooked oar, [and] you wonder that the man has not at least supplied himself with a straight one. But when with that single oar swing on one side of the boat, he sends you like an arrow on its course through the straight canals, turns corners with it, and brings you safely to his destined landing, you wonder at his skill and are humbled at your own ignorance. God uses many crooked oars, but if we yield ourselves to Him, he will bring [us] to the desired haven, and the rest during the journey is, "I know, O Lord, that the way of man is not in himself."

Who says so? The aged Christian who, humbled by his efforts and failures, looks up in faith. The young believer, who surrenders his life to the dominion of an idea: that of Christ.

The reverberations of the cannon that was fired from Fort Sumter broke the chains of millions of slaves, and still we feel individually its effect in the uncertainties of all commercial stability. A breath of wind, a sudden cold, and all the fair plans that a young man had mapped out for himself come to naught, and he finds himself a prisoner of hope, and confined in the strong dungeon of a feeble body.

The children of Israel leave Egypt, their final rest foretold by their present deliverance from slavery. Miracle follows miracle, only to [be] surpassed by a way made (through the sea) where there was no way, bitter water made sweet, bread and meat in the desert, and water from the mighty rock. In the solitariness of Mount Sinai, a God-chosen people receive God's law, with his own prophet their deliverer to declare it. Leaving behind Mount Sinai with its dread remembrance of the calf and its terrible lesson. The fiery serpents and deliverance by a look at the bronze serpent. Led by the pillar of a cloud, God's manifested presence. They come to Kadesh Barnea. Here is God smiling on his own councils—all goes well. The spies return and give glowing accounts of the country, but—the people are giants. And the people murmured and said, "Let us make a captain, and let us return into Egypt." And then when their sin is made known, they say, "Lo, we be here, and will go up unto the place which the Lord hath promised."[47]

The right use of these suggestions: Humility. Hope. Prayer. Go walk through our hospitals. Our insane asylums. Our Houses of Refuge and prisons. Read the history there of failure written on men's lives. Read "there ended" written on life's plans. And then listen. I know that the way of man is not in himself. Listen.

Except a corn of wheat fall into the ground, it abideth alone. It is the death of our life—our individualism. It is the new root of a life buried in God's will that, planted as He wills, brings forth fruit a hundredfold. The world passes by the hundredfold of gentleness and meekness, and knows not the plant, and calls it want of spirit. Passes by charity that thinketh no evil and calls it weak sentimentality. Passes by patience and long suffering, and extols the gaudy flowers of self-assertion, and cries failure to the one, and to the noxious weeds of sinful nature gives the prize. But the Lord gathers from the valley the lilies of purity and gentleness. Plucks the little pitcher plant of charity with its refreshing water for the passer by. Gathers the evergreen [that] grows rooted in the cleft of the rock and lo, they are precious in his hand, while the flowering grass of the world's treasures have faded away.

There he is—the man who did not believe this. The man that made his way in the world. "Father," he said in all the brilliancy of health, in all the pride of his vigor, in all the inpourings from without to his life, "Father, give me the portion of goods that falleth to me."[48] Whisper in the ear of that young man—stop. Oh, stop. I know that the way of man is not in himself. Can you feel the pride and sneer of that young man's heart? As if he [knew] better than that prudential father—that loving, fearful mother—that stay-at-home brother. No, others may toil if they please, but as for me—life—something will turn up. Convince that young man—no. He won't stop to be convinced. His *will* doesn't hear your words. But see—he remembers them.

He is hungry. He is poor. He is an outcast and the companion of swine. He has come to himself. "I will arise and go to my father and say, Father I have sinned and am not worthy to come under thy roof. Make me as one of thy hired servants."[49]

Where is his pride? Where his self-assertion? Now I know that the way of man is not in himself. It is to a Father—a Father's means and a Father's direction—and he finds a Father's love and success.

My friends, I know that the way of man is not in himself. It is in complete surrender to the Lord's will. It is the hearty acceptance of God's revealed truth. It is not in brain (reason) nor in affections (gratifications) nor in body (labor). It is not in man. It is of Christ, from Christ, and in Christ.

There is a way which seemeth right unto a man, but the end thereof are the ways of death. But God is the judge; he putteth down one, and setteth up another.[50]

No man can be his own successful pilot. He has not been over the way before. It must be a superior knowledge, a firmer hand, a more far-seeing eye that can guide our boat amid the storms of life, the whirlpool of our wills, past the rocks of danger, and bring us at last into the desired haven. *Faith surrenders the helm.*

CHAPTER 4

Current Events and Social Reform

Although Shipley's mind was more on the spiritual than the temporal life, the challenges and opportunities of his time nevertheless found their way into several of his sermons.

By Faith and Not by Sight was delivered on September 28, 1873, ten days after the crash of the New York Stock Market that triggered the Panic of 1873. It was a call to trust and tranquility in the midst of turbulence, and Shipley may have been preaching to himself as well. Ten years earlier, when he was only thirty-three years old, he had amassed sufficient fortune to retire from active participation in his wholesale dry goods firm.[1] However, he still maintained a share of the company,[2] and was likely worried about its future.

This sermon also refers to Professor John Tyndall, a prominent Irish physicist who gave six lectures on light while visiting America from 1872 to 1873. Unlike some of his contemporaries, Tyndall did not believe that religion and science were consistent and harmonious. He vocally supported Darwin's theory of evolution and sought to strengthen the barrier between religion and science. Yet Shipley was clearly familiar with his work, and saw in his words a suggestion that even science sometimes requires a leap of imagination beyond what can be experienced—in other words, a leap of faith.

Supplying Every Need, a sermon Shipley gave about two months later, continues with the theme of concern about the country's economy. In addition to offering reassurance about the ever-continuing life imparted by God, Shipley invokes the idea of "the one baptism" being an ongoing blessing as well. Quakers considered baptism a spiritual experience rather than a physical one (with water), and Shipley's framing of the subject—not as an event that occurred in a person's past but rather as one that is continuously ongoing through Christ—suggests that he agreed with that view. Nevertheless, the following year, while traveling in Europe,[3] he would break with that tradition and undergo physical baptism and take communion (another sacrament that Quakers considered spiritual rather than physical).[4] In response, Cincinnati Monthly Meeting would revoke his sojourning minute—a letter certifying that he was a minister of the gospel with which the Meeting was united—because they could not support such actions.[5]

By the end of 1875, when Shipley delivered the sermon *Tribulation*, the country was still in the throes of what would later be called the Long Depression. Perhaps experiencing a drop-off in business, Shipley had by then returned to active involvement in his company. Likewise, as president of the trustees of The Children's Home, he may also have noticed a drop-off in donations. While still a call to faith, this message is also a strong call to individual morality—humility, integrity, honesty, courage, and responsibility.

Tribulation also addresses the moral courage of youngsters who are honest about their schoolwork and obedience (or lack thereof) to the rules, and here Shipley was likely speaking from personal experience as a parent. At that time he had several children who were in school: Elizabeth (sixteen), Caleb (fourteen), Murray Jr. (ten), Katharine (eight), and possibly William (five).[6]

The theme of moral responsibility and following Jesus's example arises again in *Who Went About Doing Good*. This sermon is a call to action on the social reforms that Shipley perceived were needed at the time: placing orphans in families (adoption and foster care), welcoming released prison convicts, and founding institutions such as homes for incurables (hospices), coffee houses as an alternative to saloons, schools for the blind and deaf, shelters for the homeless, and hospitals for children. This message demonstrates Shipley's rejection of premillennialism—the idea that the most crucial task at hand was saving souls in anticipation of the Second Coming—and provides evidence that Shipley still embraced the traditional Quaker idea that the kingdom of God is within us, and that it is possible to help bring that kingdom into fruition in the present.

This sermon is also a paean to those who serve others—including internationally known humanitarians such as the prison reformer Elizabeth Fry and abolitionist William Wilberforce—as well as members of his own extended family. Thomas Eddy, one of the founders of the New York City public school system,[7] was the father of Ann Eddy, the first wife of Murray Shipley's father, Morris Shipley.[8] Two of Murray Shipley's maternal aunts, Mary and Anna H. Shotwell,[9] helped operate an asylum for black orphans in the 1830s;[10] the "two women" who sheltered "the friendless black orphan" likely refers to these aunts. Mary Taylor, who was particularly active in supporting indigent and vulnerable women, was the mother of Murray Shipley's first wife, Hannah D. Taylor.[11] Ephraim and Charlotte Morgan were likewise Hannah's great-uncle and great-aunt,[12] and Ephraim Morgan had been a minister at Cincinnati Monthly Meeting along with Shipley until Morgan's death in 1873.[13]

[By Faith and Not by Sight][14]

So we see they could not enter in because of unbelief.
— HEBREWS 3:19

It is not as a general thing that we cannot bear the present dispensation, not that the Lord has brought us to the point where we cannot endure at this moment, but the inability to discern the future and our fears of what may be.

It was not that God had been faithless in the past and had failed to keep [the Israelites safe in the desert] even miraculously. It was not that they were not then kept, but that they feared the future—"We be not able."[15]

It has seemed to me that this day, as well as the day a week ago, has been to many a true Sabbath, a day of rest, received thankfully by all: by those who gave no thanks to God that the excited fears of the multitude in the midst of this panic might have time to be stilled, and cooler, more collected views acted upon; and to the Christian, a day of rest, when he might renew his faith and, in the absence of corroding cares, wait upon the Lord, and renew his strength, and "go in the strength of the Lord."[16]

You may study rest in the face of an employee into whose mind has not yet dawned the fact that this panic may touch him. He goes on in fancied security, his mind is at rest because he feels his income is secure, that the loss of profits will not touch him. But this is a rest that is liable to be broken in upon at any moment. But the rest of the Christian is based upon omnipotence, omniscience, and love.

Years ago I visited Niagara Falls and went into the Cave of the Winds. My guide preceded me, and I passed over dangerous rocks and passages with his words to be watchful in my mind, until reaching a precipice, he directed me to descend a ladder and to trust him to guide my feet step by step. The winds drove the spray in blinding mists around me so that I could see nothing, but I had faith in my guide, who had been over the route himself. Turning to descend the ladder, I felt his hand on my foot, leading my foot to its right place, and then his hand on the other foot. And so, step by step, guided by his hand at the foot of the precipice, and then by his hand through the mist, he brought me out into the sunshine. And under the arch of water, I could look up and admire its beauty, and look back, and seeing the darkness through which I had come, with increased confidence (from experience) in my guide, could surrender myself to him, to follow him whither soever he might lead me. Has it not always proved so to everyone who has trusted the Lord to lead them through every blinding mist?

> So I go on not knowing;
> I would not if I might;
> I would rather walk in the dark with God
> Than go alone in the light;
> I would rather walk with Him by faith
> Than walk alone by sight.[17]

We look merely to His heart and His hand. We remain tranquil. We let our Leader care for us, and willingly follow Him upon that way in which He has not only preceded us and opened the path, but on which He is now also leading us from step to step, by His power and grace. And [He] will continue to lead us until the last step [when], attaining complete deliverance and salvation, we also pass into the same glory, where we shall behold the brightness of God in the face of His Son, our Lord Jesus Christ, and be invested with his glory. We walk by faith and not by sight.[18]

The scientist says we walk by sight and not by faith. Professor Tyndall in *Light* says, What is light? "In doing this (asking this question), we shall learn that the life of the experimental philosopher is twofold. He lives, in his vocation, a life of the senses, *using his hands, eyes, and ears* in his experiments, but such a question as that now before us carries him *beyond the margin of the senses.* He cannot consider, much less answer, the question, 'What is light?' without transporting himself to a world which underlies the sensible one, and out of which, in accordance with rigid law, all optical phenomena spring. To realize this subsensible world, if I may use the term, the mind must possess a certain pictorial power." *It has to visualize the invisible.* "This conception of the physical theory implies, as you perceive, the exercise of the *imagination.*"[19] So [Tyndall says] we are to walk by sight, not by faith, [with] the imagination that is never severed from the factual world.

[Supplying Every Need][20]

But my God shall supply all your need according to his riches in glory by Christ Jesus. — PHILIPPIANS 4:19

The man that has lived in security in a country where earthquakes do occur, but has never experienced one, is a different man after he has seen his house overthrown by one, or felt its trembling until he was willing to flee from it lest it should fall upon him. And in the present financial troubles, some houses have fallen. Some have been shaken. And while some may still stand, the lesson should be taken to our hearts of the uncertainty of all of life's gifts, to be a strong tower to us.

As I went up Glen Scraggle (near Kendal, Westmorland, England), I saw high up the mountains the bright green pastures which would be fresh when the valley was turned brown and dry. God in his nature is eternal, without beginning or ending, and in imparting of the divine nature he imparts in his gifts that ever-continuing life.

So is it in the one baptism. It was not to be a baptism which should be effective at a point of past experience and so from its *effects* good and blessing should continue to flow to the party receiving it, but it should be a baptism from which good and blessing should continue to flow *from itself*, or rather from Himself (the Holy Spirit), and be effective not at a point of past experience, but be continuously effective because continuously operative. It was not the well of water to be drank from and left behind in our journeyings, going in the strength of that water, but it was the rock rent and the water gushing forth, and that rock was Christ. It was the well of water *springing up* unto everlasting life.

There is but one saving baptism.

There is but one baptism that Christ performs.

There is but one baptism that makes us one with Christ.

[Tribulation][21]

As cold waters to a thirsty soul, so is good news from a far country.
— PROVERBS 25:25

At no time in the experience of many who are present has there been a more continuous thirst for "good news" in the restoration of general confidence, revival of active business, and relief from the pressing exhaustive effect of stagnation, inaction, and consequent suffering on the part of many classes.

The Civil War with its attendant evils brought habits of extravagant living, and at the time money seemed to be plenty in the hands of everyone. We seemed to forget that Pharaoh's seven lean kine did eat up the seven fat kine, and there was not the attention of Pharaoh to the message, nor the forethought of Joseph.[22] And as a consequence, the visitor from house to house meets with scenes of families out of work and the pinching of poverty. The benevolent institutions hear from every quarter the tale of poor business, enforced economy, and inability to aid where heretofore it has been a pleasure to give. In families there is too much an attempt to keep up appearances, while the veil is so thin that all see that it is appearances that are kept up, and not the family.

In many circles, this season of proving is bringing to view the want of principle in many business firms and individuals. Our daily papers abound with accounts of dishonorable failures and the cunning efforts of dishonest trickeries to grasp the honest gains of those who make haste to be rich, only to fall into a snare, mortify our pride as Americans, and make us demand of ourselves if it is only the lack of opportunity, or that we ourselves have not been tried by adversity, that we still stand with characters for integrity and unblemished honor.

The steam of politics has seemed to run over and carried its votaries with their false maxims and principles with every availing opportunity for money-getting. I will not say money-*making*. To do as others do seems to be a necessity for immediate success in any pursuit, and yet I rejoice there are many who recognize God as the giver of blessing to honest efforts, and by whose blessing can even the possession of acquired riches be held and enjoyed. What is demanded is retrenchment on the part of those who do not need to retrench, thus setting an example to those to whom retrenchment is really a necessity, but who may not feel the moral courage to carry out what their judgements recommend. And then the being willing to suffer any consequences rather than stoop to any actions which may weaken Christian principles and not honor the Lord.

Faith without works is dead, being alone.[23] And if there be any ghosts in this world, they certainly are the emotional feelings of the mind which cannot stand the crystalizing process of duties and trials, and so never possess a living body.

Your child in school may resist the evil example of his associates, may return honest report of his standing and obedience to the rules of the school, may quietly bear the present disadvantages he is placed under by the tricky behavior of his school fellows who fail to report their violations of school discipline. But you know that such integrity, uprightness, faithfulness on his part with its consequent lack of numerical standing is strengthening every fiber of his character and bringing him up unto true Christian manhood. But do not let us underestimate the cost he pays for this. There are those who claim that a man deserves no credit for honesty and industry—it is what he should do. But honesty and industry mean self-denial to the world, the flesh, and the devil—that is, if they spring from faith in God and the revelation of His will.

And our school boys and girls who give in the honest lower reports to their teacher than their dishonest neighbor who steals a place higher up on the list than he deserves have my commendation and are forming those habitual influences that shall crown their lives with "well done."[24]

To desire to *be* rather than to *seem* to be should be the motto of all. And in such a moment amid the trials, provings, and sorrows of life, my heart listens to, "Behold, I bring you good tidings of great joy,"[25] angelic message of good tidings from a far country to thirsty souls.

Which would be the best news—that the governor of this state had pardoned all the criminals in this state and set them free, or that all the criminals in the state were thoroughly reformed and were serving out their sentence? The gospel comes as good news—to do neither. It is to set free reformed men.

Who Went About Doing Good[26]

How God anointed Jesus of Nazareth with the Holy Ghost and with power: who went about doing good, and healing all that were oppressed of the devil; for God was with him.

— ACTS 10:38

He went about doing miracles? No. It says he went about doing good, and performed miracles. Blessed miracles—witnesses today to His power, to His deity, to his love to man. The little *children* pressed past the apostles who forbade them, and his "suffer the little children" was so easily understood by them. The *Magdalen* braved the sneer of the Pharisees, and "Thy sins are forgiven thee, go in peace" filled her heart with joy and rest. [Jesus] looked with a *look of love* [at] the young rulers, his *tears translated his heart* to the bystanders as he stood by the grave of Lazarus, and they whispered one to another, "Behold how he loved him."[27]

He lived a miracle. The miracle of a divine love reigning supreme in a human heart, and causing all to feel not only the Fatherhood of God, but the brotherhood of man.

CHAPTER 4: CURRENT EVENTS AND SOCIAL REFORM

I see one. Elizabeth Fry, leaving not her life, but the life that the world offered her, and coming down among the outcast and the prisoner, and working a miracle of reformation among the transgressors and in society, who were themselves transgressors in the manner of the confinement and punishment of criminals and debtors. I see another, John Howard, knocking at the door of Lancaster Castle to seek out [the condition of the imprisoned], and to right it.[28] I visited it myself and saw still the debtors in their confinement. I realized his work was not yet finished.

I see two more, William Wilberforce and Fowell Buxton, breaking the chains of the slave. My mind remembers two visits I paid in one day to two Johns at Rochdale, England. We all know of John Ashworth and John Bright. The one of the people, doing his work of lifting up the devil's castaways and bringing them to Christ; the other doing his work of extending the civil and religious rights of Englishmen.[29]

I see George Müller gathering his thousands of homeless orphans and teaching them love to man and trust in God, doing his work. I see Count von der Recke—[forgetting] his earthly title and going to Düsselthal—become a noble in the kingdom of God in his care of destitute children.[30] I see Mr. and Mrs. Castel with their noble son Mr. Mehle giving up their beautiful chateau and going to La Force and living among idiots, epileptics, and other incurables.

I see a small back room in the home of Thomas Eddy in New York City, a Friend, and there with him a number of the Society of Friends, and there one after another a large portion of the benevolent institutions of New York were commenced. I see two women—when to be a friend to the colored woman was to be joined to the unrecognized nobility of abolitionists—gathering into a home the friendless black orphan and carrying on the work [until the boys reached] a happy manhood.

I see Mercy Mitchell and Charlotte Morgan leading other ladies to gather the orphans in Cincinnati. I see William Crossman take the place of overseer of the poor in Cincinnati and leave in political circles the name of an honest man, and among the poor the meaning of a friend. I see Ephraim Morgan walk among his fellow citizens, the type of a single-hearted, gently loving Christian mechanic.

I see Mary Taylor spending and spent for others. I see a band of young men and women sitting among the children in the [Penn] Mission Sabbath School, with the outcasts in the prison, and in the Home for the Friendless and in the Hospital, going from house to house—anointed ones to preach deliverance to the captive.

I see the hand of the benevolent relieving the suffering of the poor and throwing wide open their hearts and doors, welcoming him or her who has few friends to their fireside. I see the strong man seizing dishonesty and hypocrisy and bringing it to the light and to justice. I see good men and women, meeting together and considering the festering wounds of society, [seeking] to raise up those who have been led astray, and yet with something of the sternness of Him who went about [with the] scourge of small cords, rebuking the manufacturers and dealers in that poison with which so many homes are today ruined, looking after the vile publications that are ruining the minds of our youth, as whiskey is their body. [I] see still God's miracles worked out by the instrumentality of those who look upon life as consisting not in the multitude of the *things he possesseth*,[31] but in the multitude of the things that he *gives*.

I have spoken of names of other countries and of other times, and some few of our own, names known to you because of their provenance. But what of the multitude which no man could number, which stood before the throne and before the Lamb, clothed with white robes and palms in their hands? These are they that came through great tribulation.[32]

Was it simply their own tribulations they came through? It was those who had learned to "bear ye one another's burdens."[33] And if we really understand that life consisteth not in the multitude of the things which we possess, but what we give, what shall I say of the many humble, fruitful lives that have been, yes, are being lived today around us, and thanks be to God in this church?

What of the mother who gave a Wesley to the world? Of that father who by his righteous life was nicknamed Righteous Christer, who gave George Fox to teach the world the soul's realization of

Christ's presence? What of the mother of Dr. Guthrie? "It was at my mother's knees that I first learned to pray." To her piety, prayers, and precepts he undoubtedly owed more than to any other human influences. Fowell Buxton writes to his mother, "I constantly feel, especially in action and exertion for others, the effects of principles early planted by you in my mind," and particularly alludes to the abhorrence of slavery and the slave trade with which she had imbued him.[34]

Far be it from me to say to anyone who feels the love of Christ constraining him to give time, heart, and life to God's especial work, but of the larger class whom Paul meant when he says, "I have shewed you all things, how that *so labouring* ye ought to support the weak," of this class to whom every morning brings its daily routine of secular duty, and the evening is their only rest—to you I desire to speak.

He went about doing good. He left us an example to follow in His steps. And He still performs miracles by His dedicated servants, however humble they may be. Into every one of your hands are committed certain talents. The courteous gentleman and lady in polished society have a smile for you, an expression of interest in what you are engaged in, a cultivated habit of shunning what would be unpleasant to you, and a happy tact of drawing you out, and you part with them, feeling the sunshine of courtesy. Now there may have been no heart in a word of it, but what they did from the habitual courtesy of good society, that you do for Christ's sake.

There are some Christians that are very much more disagreeable acquaintances than people who make no profession of religion. What do they need to pray for? To have their sins forgiven, yes, and they have need to look at that commandment, "Be courteous,"[35] and say, "Lord forgive me for being discourteous." And then to speak with a smile, and to speak about the thing the individual is interested in, and to behave as courteous as their most fashionable friend and all the time having the interior prayer of the heart looking to the Lord to cause every courteous word and act to be a sincere one, done for Christ's sake. Why, if you would keep [your love for Christ] going on for two weeks, accompanied with deeds of benevolence to go with your words where they are needed, your love would have a new lease of life.

But this is good only as far as it goes. It ought to reach your wife, children, your business, friends, and those you work for and those who work for you, but there is more still. The world is in need of miracles today. They need to say to the Christian so actively engaged in doing good, "By what authority doest thou these things, and who gave thee this authority?"[36] that the discouraged are cheered, the drunken reformed, the outcast relieved.

The orphan set in families, the sick visited, the prisoner just coming out from his confinement finds a friend, the poor consumptive taken out of her miserable room and cared for. For cripples and ruptured, [a] home for incurables.[37] Temperance refreshment rooms. A school and place of worship for the deaf and dumb, a similar one for the blind, and where such children can be taught trades adapted to their condition. The old man's home. Nightly shelter for the houseless poor. For the suppression of impure literature. Baths and wash houses for the laboring classes. Hospitals for sick children. All these need someone to be raised up who shall take one or more of these and other similar objects on his heart, shall pray for them, shall do what he can, and feel that life is given him not to acquire in but to give in, not to lay up in but to lay out, to be rich in good works.

If the objects I have mentioned today were partitioned off to persons present here, there are enough who now listen to me to found every one of these charities. Take your wealth and sow it in the ground in the shape of stones with brick and mortar on top of them, and over such a sown piece of ground gather in the halt, the blind, the maimed, the prisoner, the man ready to perish. And such an hundred fold shall be returned in time before us, as shall gladden your hearts in heaven, when the additional zero at the end of your wealth that tells you it has increased tenfold will seem of no importance to you. Now I offer you a great opportunity. Who will found a home for poor consumptives? Who a home for incurables? Who a home for discharged criminals? Who for cripples and ruptured? Who will found an industrial school and church for the deaf and dumb and blind? Who a temperance refreshment room? Who? Who? Who?

You have intelligent minds to conduct in business. Come give those powers of mind to do what He did, who will want to find something like Himself in you when He welcomes you in heaven.

Do not say you have not the wealth. I tell you, you have. If not where you can [lay] your hand upon it, God can. You have no qualifications for such work? Perhaps not—poor soul, I pity you. But there is one great comfort you can be. You may yet hear, inasmuch as you did to such one of the least [of these, you did it to me].[38]

Do you say this is mere philanthropy? No. It is philanthropy, and that means Φίλοςάνθρωπος—the love of man. And this is just the place to press upon you what Christ joined together the first and second commandment with—the work in your hand and the love of Christ in your heart. You will find God's love translated as never before as you go in his name to those that are ready to perish.

Luke 12:16 follows the parable of the rich fool. I will pull down my barns and build greater. It was possession. Not giving. It was possession and enjoying and benefit for himself. Not possession for enjoyment and benefit for others.

"The poor rich fool appears before the judgement-seat of God with a lost name, a lost soul, a lost world, and a lost heaven."[39]

For where your treasure is . . . where is it?[40] Are there not those to whom the gainings of thousands is as the gainings of hundreds, but whose givings of hundreds are harder than their former giving of thousands?

I will give thee hidden riches of secret places.[41]

CHAPTER 5

Explications

Although many of Shipley's sermons were emotional appeals to believe in and follow Christ, he occasionally offered his listeners a more scholarly approach to examining specific words or concepts—an analytical method shunned by some early Friends, but embraced by the adherents of Joseph John Gurney.[1]

Like many Quaker ministers, Shipley did not have an extensive formal education. When he was fifteen years old, he studied at St. Xavier College, a Jesuit Catholic institution that offered a Baccalaureate degree to students who completed its six-year Classical program.[2] However, he attended for only one year, perhaps due to changes in his family's circumstances. His father's lard oil business burned down in the spring of Shipley's first year at the college,[3] and he might have felt obliged to take a job to assist with the family's finances.

Nevertheless, Shipley was dedicated to furthering his own education throughout his life. He knew Greek and Latin well enough to include various words and phrases in his journal and sermons. In his preparative notes for *Lovest Thou Me. Feed My Sheep. Follow Me.* (included in Chapter 3), Shipley jotted down the different Greek words used for *feed* (to feed, to tend, to lead to pasture) as well as the different Greek words used for the animals (lambs, fully grown sheep, and weak or aged sheep in need of tender care). He also distinguished between the various Greek words for *love*. He believed that the term Jesus used, αγαπάς, was a more reverential form of love—complete, deep, eternal, the selfless love of a father. Peter's responses, φιλω, showed personal attachment—the natural affection of a child for its parent.

Shipley studied not only the Bible, but also the works of many Protestant theologians and clergymen, as well as scientists, historians, and poets whom he quotes or alludes to in his sermons.

CHAPTER 5: EXPLICATIONS

In the following messages, he assumes that his audience was likewise familiar with such men as the geologists Jean Louis Rodolphe Agassiz and Sir Roderick Murchison, as well as the English theologian Julius Hare and the writer James A. Froude. His audience was most certainly acquainted with Dr. John Warder, a member of Cincinnati Monthly Meeting who gave up his medical practice to pursue his true passion: horticulture. Warder was one of the founding members of the Cincinnati Horticultural Society and was serving as president of the Cincinnati Society of Natural History when Shipley mentioned him in his sermon *Knowledge and Power*,[4] which might have been a commencement address rather than a sermon per se. Indeed, Shipley himself embraced study of the natural world, seeing in it the mind and work of the Creator.

The sermons *Separation* and *Holiness* examine the concept of separateness from two different perspectives. In *Separation*, Shipley considers what it means for a people to be truly separated from the self, separated from the world. Embracing this type of separation leads us to greater reliance on prayer, faith, and trust; avoidance of worldly pleasures, questioning, and doubts; and freedom from anxiety. We must examine ourselves as individuals so that God might be with us as a people—providing for us when we are in need, but not necessarily protecting us from being tested.

Holiness is perhaps Shipley's harshest sermon. It focuses on the separation between a holy God and an arrogant people who believe themselves to be God's equal, dwelling on God's mercy and compassion while forgetting his purity and justice. Shipley holds up Christ as an example of sinlessness, and reminds his listeners that hell is a just end for those who sin, offering no glad tidings of the possibility of redemption.

The Love of God was delivered on Wednesday, July 8, 1874 in Liverpool, England, and appears to have been part of a weeks-long religious event. The American evangelist Dwight L. Moody was holding revivals in England, Scotland, and Ireland from 1873 to 1875, and although Moody was preaching at a separate event in London when Shipley gave his message, it was clearly common for such meetings to take place for many weeks in a row.

Expectation was likewise delivered at a special evening event, this one in support of temperance. Here he posits that half the battle is expecting to succeed, that true success might not be readily apparent, and that success also requires patience and hope in God.

Trust explores the idea that trust and faith are interchangeable concepts. We are to trust in God for our justification rather than in our own works. We are to trust God enough that we submit to his will in body, heart, and spirit. A faith that is trust brings forth spiritual fruit. (This sermon is also notable in its more marked use of Quaker language. Here Shipley explicitly refers to his efforts to deliver messages only when led by the Lord to do so at a suitable time, and that he speaks "under some measure of Light"—an indication of direct, divine revelation.)

In *Building Up*, Shipley returns to a recurring theme in his messages: the idea that sin is associated not only with debauchery, but also with self-centeredness and self-indulgence. He identifies several different classes of professed believers and the flaws in their understanding, and then systematically examines what it means to be built up in holy faith. While criticizing the outward trappings that Quakers traditionally decry (such as formality in worship, water baptism, and ordination), he nevertheless takes Friends to task for thinking that their own outward trappings (such as plain speech and plain dress) are any substitute for inner transformation.

[Knowledge and Power][5]

Lord Bacon has said, "Knowledge which man receiveth by teaching, it is cumulative." And it is this property of knowledge—to accumulate—that holds out to us all the incentive to steady application in order to develop the mental forces that his oft-quoted words "knowledge is power" may prove to be an experienced fact with each of us, bringing to us in the race of life that result which we denominate success.[6]

It is not mere masses of unapplied or misapplied power that produce the largest results. The student who degenerates into a mere bookworm has not grasped the intent of education. His mind must be awake to a perception of the principals of power that is in his knowledge with a facility and aptitude of application, if he would have the largest result of his labors. The erudite student unable to simplify and apply his accumulating knowledge to the feebler comprehension of the common mind fails of real success. Agassiz reaching alike the learned and the child is to my mind a higher type than Sir [Roderick] Murchison merely holding fellowship with the scientist.[7]

The gold washings of California. Mountain reservoirs, discharging through four pipes streams of water and washing down vast hills. We have incentives to the principal of accumulation when applied so as to bring to us its results in the shape of wealth, pressing upon us in the returns of pleasures, position, and honors. But there must be a taste created for knowledge in itself if, rejoicing in it, we shall prove to ourselves the words equally true, that knowledge is power, and that knowledge is pleasure.

I can appeal for your assent to the fact that knowledge is pleasure by the enjoyment many of you have taken in philosophy. A recent English writer expresses his satisfaction in finding the exact word to convey his thought, or to the pleasure many of you have derived from the study of the natural sciences, as they have made common things speak to you with a thousand tongues of the great Creator. My conversation with Dr. Warder about the leaf—the thought [that] Christ, knowing all things, must [have] read the wonders of the Creator's mind continually, and so been with Him in the fellowship of knowledge.

In this age that acknowledges the equality of the sexes in their common right in having access to the highest agencies for education, I need not say that, in the truth that knowledge is pleasure, I do not solely appeal to the one or the other.[8]

The Lord has willed that the mind craves a gratification which we call pleasure. But how much purer, more ennobling, and worthy are the pleasures that feed the mind than those that minister to the senses. Froude has well said, "every honest occupation to which a man sets his hand would raise him into a philosopher if he mastered all the knowledge that belonged to his craft. . . . The peasant's business is to make the earth grow food . . . yet between the worst agriculture and the best lies agricultural chemistry, the application of machinery, the laws of the economy of force, and the most curious problems of physiology."[9]

It is not a mere surface knowledge that will yield power to your character. It is knowledge in its cumulative power adding to itself those stores of wealth, that concentration of its strength, that massing of its forces. That will produce success.

The mountain reservoir is powerful in force massed and overflowing. The engine is powerful only in the might of its condensed strain. The scholar is powerful in the accretion of his knowledge. The smallest drop, the particle of steam, the first principle of the artifact are all part of the power.

On all these the lesson of patience in its Old Saxon meaning of perseverance must be incorporated in your character. And while the school life for some of you is about closing, I doubt not there has been such a taste for study formed that in your own home, your leisure moments shall find you in the best society, as Miss Faithful calls it: in the company of the best writers. May you attend to her advice: "If you do not wish to be outcasts of the best society, you must shun novels. That there be no unfurnished chambers in your mind, let there be no mental drain drinking. Dream not over the gulf that divides your aspirations and your real positions. And forget not there is a possibility of possessing true refinement in a low position, and losing it in a high one."[10]

There is, however, a higher knowledge with greater powers to which I have not alluded. Silent powers they may seem, but like the silent power of the tide and the dew, it lifts us up nearer the great heart of God and refreshes the waste heart of our fellow man and makes it green in the sense of love and sympathy.

But there is one power that the Lord gives us—it is the power of prayer. He says, "Concerning the work of my hands command ye me."[11]

> More things are wrought by prayer
> Than this world dreams of. Wherefore, let thy voice
> Rise like a fountain for me night and day.
> For what are men better than sheep or goats

That nourish a blind life within the brain,
If, knowing God, they lift not hands of prayer
Both for themselves and those who call them friend?
For so the whole round earth is every way
Bound by gold chains about the feet of God.[12]

Solomon saith, "For wisdom is a defence, and money is a defence: but the excellency of knowledge is, that wisdom giveth life to them that have it."[13] The apostle declares [in] 1 Corinthians 1:24: "But them which are called, both Jews and Greeks, Christ the power of God, and the wisdom of God."

Christ in the heart, the perennial source of power.

Separation[14]

And he said, My presence shall go with thee, and I will give thee rest. And he said unto him, If thy presence go not with me, carry us not up hence. For wherein shall it be known here that I and thy people have found grace in thy sight? is it not in that thou goes with us? so shall we be separated, I and thy people, from all the people that are upon the face of the earth.
— EXODUS 33:14-16

What separates? It is the cross of Christ that has come and has cut your life into two halves. Neither your words or mine could define the separation, as life flows in the engrossing demand on time and hand and word and thought, each performed I cannot say as of old, for we know it is not as performed faithfully. But we are conscious in the time willingly given; in the hand gladly put forth to the service; in the word spoken but attuned to the melody of His voice, who cheers the soul with His chorus of cheer, "My peace I give unto you: not as the world giveth, give I unto you. Let not your heart be troubled, neither let it be afraid";[15] in the thought that shows the separation from self, in the delicacy of Christian consideration with which the act is done.

I have thought of the various members of our Meeting, and what the several results would be upon us were such a separation realized in our experiences. I do not think it would cause any of us to be less zealous in any good work. I know that some here who have almost as pressing cares as any others are engaged in labors of love and deeds of mercy. No, I think it would make every one of us who may have done something in an effort for the salvation of souls, for the relief of distress or the alleviation of woes, bodily or spiritual, tenfold more earnest, more zealous, and more spiritual than before. While others would find a field of service—[those] whose hands had never been offered as laborers—I am sure that this would not be the main, marked change.

It would be to separate in you the spirit of your *reliances*. It would separate you to the dependence, "is it not in that thou goest with us? So shall we be separated."[16] *It would be to separate to a mighty reliance on prayer.* I believe one reason my ministry is not more blessed is it lacks the sledge blow of your prayers on the chisel of truths that I would apply to the rifted soul. I would draw you to meet together for specific objects of prayer and assail the mercy seat.

It would separate you to faith, and to lean less on agencies. It would separate you to trust when your trials came, when your plans were frustrated, when sorrow came, when partings came. It would separate you to a deep *reliance* not on things seen, but on things not seen. "Thou goest with us."

But what for you who have never given your hearts, or have looked back? All man's attempts at separation commence to work from the outside and so to the inward. But to be permanent, God's work is the reverse.

Wholly separated. Marked by "thou goest with us." [There] would not be an occasional visit to the theater or ball, would not be an evening spent in the billiard saloon, or with those with whom we could not take Christ into their company. Wholly separated would not be an indulgence in casuistical questionings and self-applauded indulgence in speculative doubts. Wholly separated would not be some transaction in business which we could not submit for Christ's signature of endorsed approbation.

It was over the road to the Promised Land that Moses said, "If thy presence go not with me, carry us not up hence." Even as Christians we need Emmanuel, God with us. How sad those that it is true of, "God is not in all thoughts."[17]

Moses wanted the Lord to go with him. Answer truly: do you want Him? Would it be convenient with your present plans, or are there some that He would be in the way? Or do you feel that you can really get along without Him?

The contrast between Moses seeking God to go with him and Adam hiding from his maker. Between Elijah rebuking a king and Elijah fleeing from a woman. "What doest thou here, Elijah?"[18]

It would be a separation from *anxiety*, temporal or spiritual. The realized presence of Christ. "All things work together." "Casting all your care." "Lo, I am with you always."[19]

In the early days of Christianity, the follower of Jesus could not conceal himself. His absence from the heathen temple, his declining the meat offered to idols betrayed him. If he kept the Lord in his heart, he was separated and known as such. Not an oath could be taken, nor an important office held without an appeal to the Romish divinities and a professed belief in them.

And not simply desiring His presence to go with us, [but] that fixing our eyes upon ourselves, we shall watch over actions that they be not evil. Remembering that Moses said, "If thy presence go not with *me*, carry *us* not up hence." It was the Lord's presence he wanted, but it was the people he had in thought.

Moses wanted the Lord's presence to control the Israelites, to supply their needs, and to guide them to the Promised Land. He wanted the Lord's presence to enforce the laws and ordinances he had just received from Him, and yet the Lord would not treat them as babes. He would give them deliverance when they were in need, would work for them at all times, but would allow them the provings of life's powers and duties.

[Holiness][20]

And one (Seraphim) cried unto another, and said, Holy, holy, holy, is the Lord of hosts. — ISAIAH 6:3

Our universal thought of Jehovah clothes him with the attribute of holiness. And yet if any of us attempt to define to our own mind what we mean by this holiness we all recognize to be the Lord's peculiar quality, each one of us would commence to define what it was not. It is to be free from sin. It is to be pure. And yet this is defining a positive virtue by negatives, or exchanging one word for another. It means separateness.

We could not recognize the holiness of any man who withheld his hand from the needy, or whose life gave evidence of any other form of selfishness. And we shall find that "holiness is only a shadow to our minds, till it receives shape and substance in the life of Christ."[21]

Are there not false conceptions in our mind of Him with whom we have to do? Do we not think of Him as a mighty ruler, but still one with whom we may argue, one with whom we may bargain? Are we not continually placing ourselves by his side, as though we had co-decision with him, and [are we not] willing to acknowledge this to ourselves? Instead of a deep sense of His omniscience and wisdom, of His omnipotence and greatness, we dwell upon his love and mercy, His compassion and patience, and forget or put out of sight and thought His holiness and justice.

While mercy and truth shall go before his face, justice and judgement are the habitation of his throne. And when on the mountain "the Lord passed by before him (Moses), and proclaimed, The Lord, The Lord God, merciful and gracious, longsuffering and abundant in goodness and truth, keeping mercy for thousands, forgiving iniquity and transgression and sin, and *that will by no means clear the guilty,*" that He is of purer eyes than to behold evil and *cannot look on iniquity*. If we thus permit the Lord to reveal Himself to us, we shall understand [that] to be holy to His holiness, He must be just to His justice—His justice to be an element in His holiness.[22]

But we must go to the life of Christ if we would understand the holiness of God. And here we have unfolded to us something of God's intention in permitting him "who was God manifest in the flesh to tabernacle among men. No man has seen God among them. The only begotten of the Father, he shall reveal him."[23]

The holiness of Christ's life challenges our attention to our high priest whom the apostle declares to be "holy, harmless, undefiled, separate from sinners, and made higher than the heavens," and to His bold words that challenge the Jews to the holiness of his life, saying, "Which of you convinceth me of sin?"[24]

Mingling continually with the daily current of life; tempted in all points yet without sin; for forty days exposed to the temptations of the devil; urged vehemently and provoked by the scribes and Pharisees to speak of many things, while they were lying [in] wait for him, seeking to catch something out of his mouth to accuse him; he remains Him who did no sin, neither was guile found in his mouth.[25]

Provision was made under the Levitical dispensation for the priest who did offer sacrifices for the people if he did sin, but no such provision for Him, the Lamb of God. And he walks through without any appearance of consciousness of sin. "He teaches His disciples to pray, 'Forgive us our trespasses.' He never prays for pardon Himself."[26]

"By the Mosaic law there was a knowledge of sin. By the teaching and example of Jesus Christ there is a much truer and deeper knowledge of it. That faultless and unapproached Life . . . endows the Christian with an ideal of sanctity (holiness) altogether His own." "It is in the *equal balance of all excellence*, in the absence of any warping, disturbing, exaggerating influence, that modern writers have been forward to recognize a moral sublimity, which they can discover nowhere in history." "He is, in short, God's answer in history to man's constant aspiration heavenward."[27]

And in the holy life of Christ, we hear from his lips, "it is better for thee to enter into life maimed, than having two hands to go into hell, into the fire that never shall be quenched." It was said [of Judas by] Jesus, good were it for that man if he had never been born. Here we see how just and true He was.[28]

[The Love of God][29]

But God commendeth (giveth proof of, sets forth, makes conspicuous) his love toward us, in that while we were yet sinners, Christ died for us.   — ROMANS 5:8

For Christ also hath once suffered sins, the just for the unjust, that he might bring us to God.   — 1 PETER 3:18

Herein is love, not that we loved God, but that he loved us and sent his Son to be the propitiation of our sins.
   — 1 JOHN 4:10

We love him (God), because he first loved us.
   — 1 JOHN 4:19

For God so loved the world, that he gave his only begotten Son, that whosoever believeth in him should not perish but have everlasting life.   — JOHN 3:16

One of the hard things for the human heart to believe is the attitude of love that God stands in towards the rebellious sinners. Still the human heart says, "We know that God heareth not sinners,"[30] but God commendeth his love, for God not only proves his love to us in Romans 5:6 ("For when we were yet without strength . . . Christ died for the ungodly"), but in this eighth verse makes it conspicuous, sets it forth, he exhibits it, he makes it the highest manifestation of the gospel.

The wonderful contrast to man's love—who would scarcely die for a righteous man—is *His* love. The consciousness of this grace-stamped love, which abode in the heart of Christ, prompted him to lay upon his disciples an injunction thus to love all. Love your enemies. "For if ye love them which love you, what reward have ye? do not even the publicans the same?"[31]

Nay, in all these things, we are more than conquerors *through him that loved us.*

To understand this feeling of love that God felt and feels towards us, think of the warmest, truest, purest love you feel for a wife, for a child, for a husband, or a parent. And then try and bestow that upon your enemy, if you have one. What do you realize? I would not do him an ill action. I would do him a kindness if I could. I don't think I hate him. I must confess, I wish I could feel a heartier interest in him. Ah! Friends, have we not all of us, you and I, [the] need today to understand—with an understanding that turns it into experience—something of that love that loved us while we were yet sinners? And proved it to us in that Christ died for us? And [what] sealing his teachings with his blood, praying "Father, forgive them" teaches us?[32] *Love* your enemies.

It is a thought. But a single thought lies at the basis of our nationality. No taxation without representation cost England her richest territory and wrote *liberty* as the watchword of our freedom.

It was but a thought. And woman awakened to her mission, and taking the weapon of all prayer goes forth to conquer the hydra-headed monster of intemperance, and closes a thousand gates to hell.[33]

A thought, but oh, such a thought as the heart of man never conceived—a revealed thought of God's heart. Love so deep that while we were yet sinners, Christ died for us.

Died for us. This is one of the hard things for the human heart to understand. Christ died for us "according to the Scriptures" is the experience of many a one who stately listens to the gospel. But what the natural man could not discern, lo, in the past few weeks, has been converted into a realized experience. And now I see responsive in your faces the answer "who loved me, and gave himself for me." Now we believe not because of thy saying, for we have heard him ourselves and know that this is indeed the Christ, the Saviour of the world.[34]

"The greatest trial and exercise of virtue is, when an innocent man submits to the imputation of a crime, that others may be free from the punishment."[35]

Oh! That we might be brought to know the inner meaning of the words "love of God."

Expectation[36]

But this man, after he had offered one sacrifice for sins for ever, sat down on the right hand of God; from henceforth expecting till his enemies be made his footstool.
— HEBREWS 10:12-13

Expecting. In all the life of the Lord, this word ever seems to be the thought of his mind in all he undertook to do. And it is the secret of half the battle. Expectation of success. He expected a successful issue to his life. Nothing more disappointing than setting before us an impossible future, or to undertake possible results by impossible means. Judged by man's judgement at the time of his death, the Lord's life was a failure. A carpenter's son, he forsook his trade, taking to a wandering life and teaching a philosophy incompatible with any earthly future to himself. He dies at the age of thirty-three with few followers, and his persecutors apparently victorious.

I was much impressed by a gentleman who visits the jail, saying of the inmates, "Their thoughts truly are not as God's thoughts, but truly they are not as our thoughts." I read over a few years ago a number of letters I wrote when I was just approaching manhood, and I could not have believed I ever felt, thought, and acted as those letters brought back my old self.

There [is] no laborer who has tried to reach down a hand to any sunken in the mire of sin that has not heard the sad tones, "It is no use my trying, I cannot." Noah's life and pursuits in building the ark were stamped with failure in the eyes of many who saw the ark building.

Expectation embraces looking for, waiting for. The Lord did not expect his enemies to be made his footstool until *"after* he had offered one sacrifice for sins," and only when we accept this offering can we have a right to *expect*.

He expected some men would not listen, some would gladly hear and only endure [until] trial came, some sneer, and some persuaded. But strong in his knowledge of the future, he went on, and strong he waits and looks for his enemies to be made his footstool.

Columbus looking for the *new world*.

I do not know but that this night, this spirit of expectation fills more minds than ever before. And it is this spirit of expectation that sends us with the prayer of faith to His ear that is ever open to make known our requests, believing—expecting. "But if we hope for that we see not, then do we with patience wait for it."[37]

The word *patience* does not occur in the Old Testament. *Patient* only in Ecclesiastes 7:8, and *patiently* only in Psalm 37:7 and 40:1. Not that it was not known, for [in] James 5:11, "Ye have heard of the patience of Job."

"And now, Lord, what wait I for? my hope is in thee."[38]

[Trust][39]

Blessed is the man that trusteth in the Lord, and whose hope the Lord is. For he shall be as a tree planted by the waters, and that spreadeth out her roots by the river, and shall not see when heat cometh, but her leaf shall be green; and shall not be careful in the year of drought, neither shall cease from yielding fruit.

— JEREMIAH 17:7-8

I have reverently sought of the Lord His guidance, that I might be kept by Him as His messenger to deliver to you such applications of His truth as He sees is suited and suitable at the time.

Under some measure of Light two weeks ago I brought to your view (and to the view particularly of the children) the subjects of honesty and industry. Honesty as it represents self-denial to the world, the flesh, and the devil; industry as it stands for patient continuance in well-doing; and both representing acts of faith, doing what we do heartily unto the Lord and not unto man.[40]

And last week I set before you the obedience of faith.[41] Obedience as it represents submission to authority and compliance with command or prohibition—Christian obedience as it implies faith which worketh by love. Not that obedience which *gives up* so much that the heart would like *to keep*, to obtain what is believed to be a necessity. Not the miser parting with his gold for bread, not the voluptuary parting with his pleasures for health's sake, not the half-hearted professor of Christianity parting with the amusements and frivolities of life to escape the stings of conscience, but such an obedience as the Lord defines. I seek not mine own will, but the will of the Father which hath sent me.[42] Here is surrender, consecration, and faith—and this is Christian obedience.

There are some can tell the trees from their forms, some from their bark, some from their leaves, but all can tell them by their fruit—"by their fruits ye shall know them"—and so we have been looking at some of the fruits of the tree of life. Honesty. Industry. Obedience. Today I want us to realize how we are or can be made "fruit-bearing branches."[43]

The text from Jeremiah 17:7-8—"Blessed is the man that trusteth in the Lord, and whose hope the Lord is. For he shall be as a tree planted by the waters, and that spreadeth out her roots by the river, and shall not see when heat cometh, but her leaf shall be green; and shall not be careful in the year of drought, neither shall cease from yielding fruit."—is drawn by the prophet as a contrast to the fifth and sixth verses: "Cursed be the man that trusteth in man, and maketh flesh his arm, and whose heart departeth from the Lord. For he shall be like the heath in the desert, and shall not see when good cometh; but shall inhabit the parched places in the wilderness, in a salt land and not inhabited."[44]

From the time that Boaz uses the word to Ruth—"under whose wings thou art come to trust"—we find the word *trust* constantly repeated. Job says [in] Job 13:15, "Though he slay me, yet will I trust in him." David constantly stays up his heart: "I trust in thee." "They that trust in the Lord shall be as mount Zion." Isaiah again and again encourages to trust: "Who is among you that feareth the Lord, that obeyeth the voice of his servant, that walketh in darkness, and hath no light? Let him trust in the name of the Lord, and stay upon his God." [In] Jeremiah 49:11, Jeremiah is the messenger who says, "Leave thy fatherless children, I will preserve them alive; and let thy widows trust in me." Nahum 1:7 says, "The Lord is good, a strong hold in the day of trouble; and he knoweth them that trust in Him." And of our Savior it is declared, "And in his name shall the Gentiles trust."[45]

CHAPTER 5: EXPLICATIONS

And recently in England, one of the best scholars in our Society presented before me the propriety and possibility of generally substituting the word *trust* for the word *faith* in the New Testament. And it is faith that is trust that I desire to present to you today.

Yet looking over this congregation, there are some who, if I was to be with them in privacy—I should say now faith comes by hearing—I should press upon them Luther's great text, Christ's first sermon: "The kingdom of God is at hand: repent ye, and believe the gospel." To such here who are inclined to a mystical spiritualizing away [of] the great doctrine of being justified by faith (we have peace with God through our Lord Jesus Christ), who understand good works, pure lives, and rest their inner trust on these—to such I would say, "So ye conclude that a man is justified by faith without the deeds of the law." And I earnestly crave I may so present to you the claims of faith or trust [that] you may see it embraces trust in the gospel and trust in Him who was the messenger of the gospel.[46]

I claimed of you that obedience meant obedience of or from the three sides of man's nature: body, mind, and spirit. And faith, the spring of obedience, thus lays claim on the whole of man, which is fairly represented by one word: *will*.

Are there those here who reply, You say believe in the Lord Jesus Christ and thou shall be saved, and I do believe and have always so believed from my childhood? Ah, how far have you allowed truth to take hold of you? Has it seized your body, and you have yielded that as you have yielded the assent of your mind? Has it infused your spirit, so that your affections center around the truth? Has it seized the stronghold of the man—the will—and in truth you say with Christ, "I seek not my own will, but the will of the Father which hath sent me"?[47]

And the other class, who do yield their body in obedience but whose affections are [only] in some measure on Christ—do you yield your minds to the truth, unhesitatingly casting out all reasonings on the naked declaration of God's words: "And by him all that believe are justified from all things, from which ye could not be justified by the law of Moses."?[48]

Does God see us today who are gathered before Him having the truth hid from us or revealed unto us? He hides His truths from the wise and prudent, and reveals them unto babes. Except ye be converted, and become as little children, ye shall not enter into the kingdom of heaven.[49] Little children wait to be taught by their parents. Humility. They *believe* what they are told with their minds. A *faith* which works by love moves their spirits, thus affections. A *trust* that prompts to action produces dedication of their bodily powers and thus, the will in healthy exercise is moved upon. And in word, thoughts, and deeds, a faith that is trust and based in belief brings forth fruit.

Archdeacon Hare well says, "For Faith, and Faith alone, gives us the very thing which Archimedes wanted, the standing-place out of the world, and above the world, whence the world is to be moved."[50]

Is it then the action of mind, body, and spirit by which the soul, by the exercise of will, becomes and remains a Christian? Let me again quote from Hare: "The flower must open by an act of its own, before the sunbeams can enter into it: and though it opens under the warmth of those very rays, which, before they gain an entrance, lie fosteringly around it, still, unless there was a living principle in the plant, the warmth of the sun would no more unfold the blossoms, than it can open an artificial bud, or a painted one."[51]

The original meaning of one of the Hebrew words used for trust is *to cling*. It is the word used for a child clinging to its mother's breast. "To run for shelter," the meaning of another Hebrew word. "To lean upon," another Hebrew word from which the word *amen* is derived.

So though faith comes by hearing, "There must be some motion of the Will, however slight, which in the first instance directs the application of the Understanding to an object, before that object can be introduced through the Understanding to act upon the Will." "Hereby we may be assisted in some degree to conceive how the influences of the Spirit should be of such momentous power in the work of our Faith—in producing it from the very first, and afterwards in nourishing and maturing it."[52]

CHAPTER 5: EXPLICATIONS

[Building Up][53]

How that they told you there should be mockers in the last time, who should walk after their own ungodly lusts. These be they who separate themselves, sensual, having not the Spirit. But ye, beloved, building up yourselves on your most holy faith, praying in the Holy Ghost, keep yourselves in the love of God, looking for the mercy of our Lord Jesus Christ unto eternal life.
— JUDE 1:18-21

As ye have therefore received Christ Jesus the Lord, so walk ye in him: rooted and built up in him, and stablished in the faith, as ye have been taught, abounding therein with thanksgiving.
— COLOSSIANS 2:6-7

Let your light so shine before men, that they may see your good works, and glorify your Father which is in heaven.
— MATTHEW 5:16

In Jude 1:18-19 and 20-21, the apostle (Jude) draws a great contrast. These be they who separate themselves, *sensual*, not having the Spirit, mockers (scoffers) who should walk after their own *lusts*; and ye beloved, keeping yourselves in the love of God, by "*building up* yourselves on your most holy faith," by "praying in the Holy Ghost," by looking for (waiting for) the mercy of our Lord Jesus Christ.

Of the first class: walking after their own *lusts*. *Sensual*. These words we are apt to apply to grosser sins, and so pass over them as not applicable to ourselves. The word *lust* means "eagerness to possess or enjoy," as lust of gain or of pleasure. And the word *sensual* is several times rendered *natural*. The natural man discerneth not the things of God, for they are spiritually discerned. It means the man who is not spiritual, the man in whom the earthly life of the soul reigns. He who thinks of self and self-interests. "These are our Epicureans and Sadducees, who believe neither one thing nor the other, who live as they think best and walk after their own lusts, considering permitted whatever suits their pleasure: examples of such are met on every hand."[54]

No more common form of expression is on the lips of men, in any discussion on religious subjects, than "I believe." The irreligious respectable man, from the man who says, "I believe preachers are a set of hypocrites" to the man who says, "I believe the Bible and in the existence of God and of the death of Christ, but I think God has given me certain faculties and powers, and He intends I should use them and enjoy them. And if I do so rightly, I'll get to heaven as well as those who profess so much about faith and live out very imperfect lives."

In the Lord's providence I have been thrown the past week with a large body of men (at Columbus), the lives of some of whom are grossly evil and sensual. Others whose aim, judged by a worldly standard, are good. And others still whose purposes are to live for Christ. Those who make sweeping assertions against professors of religion are generally themselves not infallible in their own lives, and who cover their own gross derelictions from morality with "I make no profession," as if that excused them.

Others give a nominal assent to Christianity but, if they were honest to themselves, would own that their own purposes as evinced by their daily life was to gain in wealth, honor, position, or pleasure, and to use their time so that it should render a return that should be to their gain. Probably with such a life might be some occupation of time for the good of others, an honest life so far as the practices of ordinary business life are taken, or a standard who were virtuous, good husbands and fathers and sons, but to whom faith as a blessed assurance of eternal trust and joy is unknown.

The third class [are those] who profess to be Christians and are, but whose consciences continually reproach them for their deadness [and] worldliness, but yet in whose heart is the assurance that the live coal from the holy altar has touched their lips, and their sins are forgiven.

There is a fourth class—and I rejoice in believing that they worship here this morning—upon whom the magnet of Christ's love is continually a drawing power, and who recognize in the exhortation of the apostle a parallel to their own experience. In their aim to keep themselves in the love of God. In building up. In praying. In looking for.

CHAPTER 5: EXPLICATIONS

How many here *walk after* their *own lusts*? We are exhorted to build up ourselves on our most holy faith. What a strong contrast. Those who are walking after their own lusts are building up themselves in their most ungodly lusts. Those who are building up themselves on that most holy faith are walking after the most holy faith—notice the contrast—their *own*.

Separate themselves. What a terrible separation. To their lusts, to their own sensual natures. Look at the contrast. "Keep yourselves in the love of God." Paul in Romans 1:1 calls himself an apostle separated to the gospel of God. What a contrast [between] "their own ungodly lusts" and "God's love" (love of God).

A walk after our *own ungodly lusts* leads us among persons and things of a similar character. (Christians walk through *Vanity Fair.*) In contrast, in Romans 8:1, "There is therefore now no condemnation to those of them which are in Christ Jesus, who walk not after the flesh, but after the Spirit."

But here is the clear instruction to us to an end. The object (on the basis of a *possessed faith*) is keeping ourselves in God's love. Everyone. The means—building. Praying. Looking for.

For other foundation, "let every man take heed how he buildeth thereupon."[55] Here is the basis, the foundation, and other foundation can no man lay than that which is laid by God's hand for man to build on. Build on the sands of human works, human thoughts—they are like man's acts, they have no cohesion, the torrents shall tear them away. Gather a handful of sand and step into the ocean and attempt to lay a foundation for a lighthouse with it. And as the sand is lowered into the waves, lo, it is gone. Nothing but a rock for a sure foundation. And none other than the rock, Christ Jesus. (No rolling stone like Peter.)

But take heed how you build on that foundation, and yet we are exhorted, "building up yourselves on your most holy faith." It is a preacher's exhortation, how we add opinions to holy opinions, but opinions—faith—express themselves in actions. Look at the beautiful work of Palissy the potter, of Jean Goujon, both Protestants, and one dying for his faith in the massacre of St. Bartholomew. See how their thought without a model is executed. See the different schools of thought, science, art, and manufacture, with perhaps a common faith, building thereon these opinions which they expressed in form and which remain or are passed behind the curtain of the mists of forgotten deeds.[56]

Look at the true faith of the apostolic teaching, with a superstructure of Roman superstitions in forms, relics, and traditions, until on the foundation of a true faith has risen a trust in ceremonies, in a ritual, in the reliance of the heart on outward ordinances as God's way of approaching the soul instead of access by faith through Christ.

Has thou faith in Christ? Let the world see how faith is manifested by works. And upon the foundation, let the world *see the superstructure*, and if it be without a *crack*, then will they believe in such a foundation. But if thou build of untempered mortar, then shall the foundation be criticized with what was the fault of the material of the superstructure. They who teach for doctrine the commandments of men.

The extreme unction—the mass among Romanists. Forms of speech and dress among Friends. Being baptized in water, producing baptismal regeneration. The laying on of hands, ordaining the minister by giving of the Holy Ghost. The duty of benevolence as though in the money given, instead of the love to Christ being therein represented. And in like manner philanthropic labors done merely from duty, and not done as a duty that love prompted. All then are but gold, silver, precious stone—wood, hay, and stubble, which shall be burned, and we suffer loss. Whereas the original design of which these things were the outward sign, if done from the power of *life* reigning in the soul, are no longer dead works, but rather of such [that] God is not unrighteous to forget your works (of love) and labors of love.[57]

We follow to the grave those who are dear to us. And the question of eternity, as we part with those we love, ceasing to be simply a question of the *mind* merely, becomes the great question of the *heart*. And at such a time the soul feels the need of building up itself on the most holy faith.

One manner of building up ourselves is the faithful carrying out [of] little matters of conscientious faith. They that do His will shall know of the doctrine, and it is as faith is reduced to practice [that] we gain clear, sharp views of truth. [If] Watt—who discovered the power of steam by the moving of a kettle lid—or any great discoverer [could] look down the vista of a century and know the fullness of the power of his discovery, how would his faith in it be increased.

Read God's answers to *His promises*, so will you build up yourself in our most holy faith. By resolutely putting away doubts. By *taking heed*. By acknowledging some questions as to the existence of sin and similar questions to be beyond the finite grasp of our minds. By searching the Scriptures daily and feeding upon them, using them not as a tuning fork to key up our emotions, but feeding upon the promises and drawing out for ourselves fresh treasures from this storehouse of spiritual riches. By realizing that skeptical doubts never bring a settled assurance of a future condition, while faith in Christ does. By meditation. Retirement.

Not every stone when first taken from the quarry is ready for the building. The diamond, when found, needs to be polished. And crude thoughts, even from the Scriptures, need to be proved and prayed over and waited for. Burn your own smoke, and let the stone be squared and the diamond polished.

And there is need of building up yourselves, for the old man lies in ruins, and it is the new man that needs to be builded up. It is eternal life commenced that is to be builded.

By a public avowal of your faith.

By that moderation which evidences the control of the Spirit and that zeal that shows His quickening power.

By private and family prayer. By prayerful listening to the truth preached. Taking someone else in prayer while the truth is preached.

The compass is constantly consulted.

CHAPTER 6
Exhortation

In *A Description of the Qualifications Necessary to a Gospel Minister*, Bownas noted that one of the primary functions of preaching was "to stir up the believers to remember their duty." Indeed, many of Shipley's sermons address the duties of his listeners: to love God and one another, to pray, to be diligent and bold in their faith, to recall with humility that all are equal in the eyes of God, and to live lives transformed through grace.[1]

In *Loving the Lord*, a sermon that encourages Friends to observe the greatest commandments and to engage in family devotions, Shipley describes David the psalmist as "advancing in his Christian experience." Although Shipley certainly knew that David was a Jew, this phrasing reflects the traditional Quaker perspective that the seed of Christ exists in all people, even those who lived before the birth of the historical Jesus.[2]

More surprising is his suggestion that his listeners should have a family altar. Although the *Book of Discipline* that guided Quaker faith and practice during that period encouraged families to read the Bible and pray together, it discouraged formality in doing so.[3] It is possible that in discussing the use of an altar, Shipley was speaking metaphorically rather than literally. His granddaughter recalled that in his own home, every member of the family, their servants, and any household guests gathered to pray and recite a verse of Scripture every day after breakfast in the home's library.[4]

Although it was not uncommon for Quaker ministers to receive feedback on their messages, in *Loving the Lord*, Shipley speaks of criticism as the "bane of the minister's life." In this particular instance, he might have been reacting to criticism that he perceived as both unduly harsh and indiscreet, since it seems to have occurred in front of children (perhaps his own). Nevertheless, his own reaction—to publicly claim that such words came from "cold hearts not touched by the love of Christ"—was likewise harsh. Bownas specifically warned ministers to "[keep] a close watch over thy own temper and spirit, lest prejudice should beget hard thoughts in thy mind against those whom thou mayest look upon as opposers . . . so that if thou art of a vindictive temper, and apt to resentment, this may, if thou art not very watchful, tincture thy ministry with bitterness, which will appear by giving slant and side strokes to thy preaching, or by suffering thyself to think, that what they offer in opposition . . . proceeds from some private pique or resentment, and not from any just cause of objection that they have to thy ministry." Indeed, Shipley may well have had to spend time mending fences with both his critic and his Meeting after delivering what was an otherwise sound and encouraging message.[5]

Although *Loving the Lord* was delivered in Cincinnati, *Not Ashamed* was given in Kent, England, while Shipley and several members of his family were living abroad.[6] His words reflect an awareness of his more reserved and privileged British audience. Here Shipley contrasts the outspoken courage of the apostle Paul to proclaim the gospel when it was counter-cultural to do so with the tepid embarrassment of the gentry who do not want to appear too religious or to admit that they need redemption. (Shipley's demure assertion that some of the school boys in the audience were not ashamed of the gospel may well have been a nod to his own youngsters. During this trip, two of Shipley's sons—thirteen-year-old Caleb and nine-year-old Murray Jr.—attended the Friends School in Kendal, England.[7])

In *Not Ashamed*, Shipley also shows that he might have shared a perspective common among those of Western European descent regarding individuals "who have not lived in a civilized community"—a phrase that could have encompassed all non-white indigenous people. Such people, according to Shipley, were not ashamed of their way of life until presented with a "better" one, implicitly a Western one, at which point they would be "ashamed of the old and strive for the new." By speaking in such terms, Shipley departs from the best of Quaker tradition. When the eighteenth-century Friend John Woolman traveled among Native Americans, he hoped that he "might feel and understand their life and the spirit they live in," and that he "might receive some instruction from them, or they might be in any degree helped forward by [his] following the leadings of truth among them."[8] By being open to learning about and from Native Americans, Woolman demonstrated respect for them even as he was led to share his own experiences with them. Shipley, who since 1871 had been serving on the Associated Executive Committee of Friends on Indian Affairs,[9] would have done well to emulate Woolman's approach.

In *No Difference*, Shipley reminds his audience that those who live moral, middle-class lives are no better in the eyes of God than the reprobates who fill the city's slums. Indeed, if anyone merits mercy, it is those with the least advantages.

In *Repentance*, Shipley reiterates that all people need to acknowledge and confess their sins, to seek mercy, and to lead changed lives as a result of receiving grace.

[Loving the Lord][10]

Hear, O Israel: The Lord our God is one Lord: and thou shalt love the Lord thy God with all thine heart, and with all thy soul, and with all thy might. And these words, which I command thee this day, shall be in thine heart: and thou shalt teach them diligently unto thy children, and shalt talk of them when thou sittest in thine house, and when thou walkest by the way, and when thou liest down, and when thou risest up.
— DEUTERONOMY 6:4-7

The Lord [Jesus] repeats the first great command: "And thou shalt love the Lord thy God with all thy *heart*, and with all thy *soul*, and with all thy *mind*, and with all thy *strength*; this is the first commandment."[11] And what so fulfills the second great command—to love our neighbor as ourselves—as to talk of his words and teach them, having them in *our hearts*?

And when the psalmist would describe the righteous, he saith, "The law of his God is in his heart; none of his steps shall slide." And expressing his own experience he says, "thy law is within my heart." And as he advances in Christian experience he says, "Thy word have I hid in mine heart, that I might not sin against thee." "Thou through thy commandments hast made me wiser than mine enemies."[12]

I am glad that it was our Lord and Savior who said *mind*. Thou shalt love the Lord thy God with *all* thy mind. And the lawyer answers, "Well, Master, thou hast said the truth: for there is one God; and there is none other but he: and to love him with all the heart, and with all the *understanding*, and with all the soul, and with all the strength, and to love his neighbor as himself, is more than all whole burnt offerings and sacrifices." And the narrative goes on to say, "And when Jesus saw that he *answered discreetly* (with knowledge and understanding), he said unto him, Thou art not far from the kingdom of God."[13]

And while Christ teaches that "love is the fulfilling of the law," he teaches faith first. The Lord is one Lord, for he that cometh to him (to love him) must first believe that He is. And I showed you a few Sabbaths [ago] that Christ included in his query of Simon—"Lovest thou me?"—his earlier lessons of faith in "Whom say ye that I am?" and hope in "Could ye not watch with me one hour? Watch and pray."[14]

"The [true] measure of loving God is to love Him without measure." "The measure of love to man: our love to ourselves."[15]

"Thou shalt teach them diligently." Adam Clarke [defined this as to] "repeat, iterate, or do a thing again and again, hence to whet or sharpen any instrument, which is done by reiterated friction or grinding." Diligence. "It requires much patience, much prudence, much judgement, and much piety."[16]

Shall *neglect* be the source of sorrow in [the] future, and the charge against you be neglect?

"Thou shalt" as thou sittest in *thy* house. Here certainly parents are taught to teach intelligently to their children. His words, which they are to have in their "own hearts." Can the father or mother do this who have no family altar in the home, who never teaches diligently day by day the use of the Scriptures, by reading it in connection with devotion, impressing its truths intelligently upon the minds of his children, and teaches how he values the Scriptures by this public example to his children of reading it diligently with them? Can the parent teach his children honesty and purity and unselfishness and love to his neighbor and duty to parents who never opens his lips to them on these subjects? Nor does not set them the example, showing both by precept and example, here a little and there a little, his own heart's confidence in them?

And can you suppose you are doing all that you should do to be counted diligent if your words and example do [not] inculcate the duty of *prayer*? If the family altar is neglected, or if it is only to be remembered by your children as the place where a few verses of Scripture were daily read—good as this is—if there is not to be garnered in their minds the memories of times when their own hearts went up with the father's or mother's supplications, and it may be, that altar remembered where under a father's or mother's ministrations or prayers, they gave their hearts to the Lord Jesus?

And what is to be thy own condition of heart? Love with heart and soul and mind and strength. A burning, earnest love. A love that tenders us, makes us gentle, watchful in speaking, drawing by love, going before and constraining by the drawings of love, carrying the lambs in our bosom, our own faith and our own love being strength and warmth of heart to them.

And there is no escaping the plain meaning of these words. If it be said we are to teach them diligently to our children, by example and look and circumspection of life—that there are other ways of confessing the Lord than by speaking, I accept all these ways as being incumbent and not to be escaped from—but the Lord says, "Thou shalt *talk* of them when thou sittest in thine house," etc. And here is just the word—our hearts should so feel His cause first. We are to *talk* about it when we *sit* in our houses, that the children shall come to feel that religion is the first great object of life, because their parents are constantly talking about it and always carrying it out.

When Jesus, dying on the cross, saw his mother and the disciple standing by whom he loved, he saith unto his mother, "Woman, behold thy son!", then said [to] the disciple, "Behold thy mother!"[17] And from that hour that disciple took her unto his own home. What are your thoughts of that home? The mother of Jesus and disciple Jesus loved.

Mother, do you forget your dear one whom the Lord has taken to him? Have you lost a friend that was the one whom your soul leaned on? Could you live in the home of his mother and never speak of him?

But how often, however, the Lord must have been the theme of conversation in that home. His cause. The last accounts from Peter and Paul, from Apollos and Barnabas. The last [word] they had of Paul in his journeying. The work of the Lord, how it was prospering. Instances of conversion. Means to be used. The words of the Lord Jesus. United prayer of the mother and her new son for the cause's sake. How they must have gone to the place of worship together. "These all (the disciples) continued with one accord in prayer and supplication, with the women, and Mary the mother of Jesus, and with his brethren."[18] After the day of Pentecost and times of refreshing, how the song of thanksgiving went up from many hearts.

That bane of the minister's life—criticisms of cold hearts not touched by the love of Christ, criticisms in conversation in the presence of the children and of other tender-hearted ones—never fell from lips that were only full of the sense of redemption, of its need of promulgation. Talk to your children, but oh, put no such stumbling blocks in their way. Talk of His laws, talk of His love, talk of His work in your own soul and that of others, talk of the need of children to give their hearts to Jesus now.

How [Jesus's mother and His disciple] must have spoken of the persecutions and encouraged one another. How they must have thanked God for Paul's conversion. Do you say times are changed? Ah! It is because you are not joined into the service of the Lord.

On what ground did the Lord claim the entire love and obedience of the children of Israel? "I am the Lord thy God, which have brought thee out of the land of Egypt, out of the house of bondage." "That it may be well with thee." And the apostle tells us [in] Galatians 2:20: "And the life which I now live . . . I live by the faith of the Son of God, who loved me, and gave himself for me."[19]

And on this ground He claims us—"who loved me, and gave himself for me." Christ, *who loved me and gave himself for me.*

[Not Ashamed][20]

For I am not ashamed of the gospel of Christ: for it is the power of God unto salvation to every one that believeth; to the Jew first, and also to the Greek. For therein is the righteousness of God revealed from faith to faith: as it is written, The just shall live by faith.

— ROMANS 1:16-17

It was not a man of merely emotional feeling moving, as we do, in a community where it is respectable to profess the faith of Christ. But it was one who had not shrunk from opposition and persecutions, and who had proved the gospel to be in truth the power of God. Realize, if you can, the magnificence and power of Rome at this [time]. The mistress of the world, proud of her victories, her heroes, and her gods. Steeped in brutality and mad with crime. Her liberty a name and her religion licentiousness, and you comprehend something of the outlook when Paul said, "I am ready to preach the gospel to you that are at Rome also."[21]

It is but a few weeks since I was on the shores of the Mediterranean where Paul landed at Puteoli. There are still the remains of the temple of Serapis and the Amphitheater where bloody combats were the delight of women as well as men. Near it was Baiae with its temple of Mercury, Diana and Venus. The very religion of the country gratifying to the low instincts of the natural man found its expressions in the temples themselves in unbridled profligacy.

It was to overthrow the most showy, sensual, and strongly footed religions [that] this man Paul turned his face toward Rome and said, "I am not ashamed of the gospel of Christ: for it is the power of God unto salvation." Ah, well for us he was not ashamed of it. He had never been put to shame by it. His had been a march of victory. What was wiser than the wisdom of Greece, was stronger than the might of Rome? Christ, the wisdom of God and the power of God. Today we reap the benefits of that brave man's life. I am not ashamed of the gospel of Christ—who feels this? Man, woman, boy, or girl?

CHAPTER 6: EXHORTATION

Not ashamed to be called an Englishman, German, American. Men who have not lived in a civilized community are not ashamed of their wants of comfort and their low standard of intelligence and comfort, but when a knowledge of a better life with greater advantages arising from it has quickened their thoughts, they are ashamed of the old and strive for the new.

In the community in which we live, we are not ashamed [of] some of the fruits of the gospel of Christ—pure morality, perfect integrity, unselfish and philanthropic lives. And yet [some] are ashamed of the gospel. Persons are not ashamed in this world to be rich by inheritance. The possession of inherited wealth and position is generally a matter of pride. Who is thus ashamed of his wealth or his native powers of mind? And yet "the glad tidings" speak of a message received in the heart of God's love. Christ's redemption, forgiven sin, heart union with the Lord, and a separated life.

It is not, "I am not ashamed of a religious or moral life of integrity." The man easily prides himself in his powers of mind, his philanthropy, his good name. He looks down upon the man who cannot deny himself that which injures him. He prides himself in his honesty. But Paul says, "God forbid that I should glory, save in the cross of our Lord Jesus Christ, by whom the world is crucified unto me, and I unto the world." Notice Paul was not ashamed of a trust in that which was opposed to the prevailing trust of the world and its modes of thought. A trust that accepted of free grace, the glad tidings of salvation as to faith ("from faith to faith"—to faith and for faith).[22]

What do the statesmen today think of the gospel of Christ? Little or nothing. The scientist—nothing. The fashionable world— nothing. The school boy—I will not say nothing, for I am convinced it is otherwise with some who are present. The father. The teacher. The merchant. The apprentice. The boy. The girl.

[No Difference][23]

For there is no difference: for all have sinned, and come short of the glory of God.   — ROMANS 3:22-23

But we believe that through the grace of the Lord Jesus Christ we shall be saved, even as they.   — ACTS 15:11

For whosoever shall call upon the name of the Lord shall be saved.   — ROMANS 10:13

These words of the two great speakers come to us as messages fraught with deep instructions. Messages to show us our real condition before the Lord. There is no difference. Jew or Gentile, rich or poor, for all have sinned and come short of the glory of God. Sinners before him, sinners dead in trespasses and sins, sinners with the Lord's own words sounding in our ears: except we [be] born again, we cannot enter into the kingdom. Sinners with the message: except ye repent, ye shall all likewise perish—perish![24]

As it was in the days of Noah, they ate, they drank, they were married and were given in marriage, until the day that Noah entered into the ark and the flood came and destroyed them all. Likewise also as it was in the days of Lot. They did eat, they drank, they bought, they sold, they planted, they builded, but the same day that Lot went out, it rained fire and brimstone from heaven and destroyed them all.[25]

Sinners, we have all sinned. No difference. All the world guilty before God. Therefore by the deeds of the law shall no flesh be justified before God. But the scripture hath concluded all under sin, that the promise by faith of Jesus Christ might be given to them that believe.[26]

All sinners. No difference. How offensive! No difference between the man whose life has been devoted to the good of his fellow man, whose moral habits and self-denying life are an incentive to those who know him to refrain from [the] sins of life about them? No difference between such a man—intelligent, moral, self-denying, benevolent, and philanthropic, but who has not sought God in the forgiveness of sin—and the brutal, low, ignorant, selfish, and debased sinner? No difference? The Bible says so. Ah, if there is to be a difference—as a dear Christian lady once said to me—with all our advantages, education, influences, culture, when I walk through our slums and see how from their very infancy [the youngsters are] taught to drink, taught to swear and lie and steal, taught by their parents and trained up for habits of sin and immorality—oh, if there ought to be a difference, it would seem it should be made for these, and that we who have had careful instruction, to whom the revelation of God has been an accessible book, we should well need to listen.

I will send the Comforter, and he will reprove the world of sin, because they believe not on me. For God hath concluded them all in unbelief, that he might have mercy upon all.[27]

Repentance[28]

What new doctrine is this? — MARK 1:27

They were astonished at his doctrine. — MARK 1:22

My doctrine is not mine, but his that sent me.
— JOHN 7:16

Behold the Lamb of God, which taketh away the sin of the world.
— JOHN 1:29

[John the Baptist] said *the kingdom of heaven is at hand* to the repentant sinners. He said *wrath to come* to the Pharisees and Sadducees. The professor and not possessor, and the free thinker and moralist.[29]

The act of the repentant: confessing their sins. Showing their deeds, earnestly acknowledging their sins were their own. Repentance. Change of mind. Afterthought. Reflection.[30]

Free repentance implies a consciousness, defined or undefined, of utter helplessness. A person struggling for his life in the water does not consciously define to himself his position. He is conscious of his helplessness and cries, "Save, or I perish!" "Father, I have sinned," [said the] prodigal [son]. "I have sinned," [said] David. "God be merciful to me, a sinner."[31]

The charge to the repentant: bring forth therefore fruits meet for repentance. *Behold the Lamb of God*.[32]

There is going to come a time when probably you will be alone in your bed with the footstep of one approaching your bedside, when the one that loves you most cannot keep away. You feel your singleness. There you lie, and his cold hand is about to be laid upon you. Are you alone? Yes, as far as the power of human love can go. Your feet touch the brink of the river. Do you feel its waters? Are they cold, and does your hand chill? Are you going to go *down* into the waters *alone*? Or shall the waters divide as by the touch of one of the Lord's priests, and you pass through dry shod saying, "When I pass through the valley of the shadow of death, I will fear no evil: for *thou art with me*?"[33]

McCheyne says, "A man may be able to change his sins, but, ah! what man can change his heart?"[34]

Some years since I was visiting with a city missionary (Mr. White) through the poorer districts of Spitalfields in London. In a miserable dark room we found a woman very poor. Her room bore some marks of taste, but it was not nearly so clean and neat as some poorer rooms we had entered. Her dress was tawdry, yet she had a small piece of fine lace in the cap she wore. She commenced at once with this scrap of lace as a basis, and talked of "my Lady" with whom she once lived as an upper servant. Her life thus seemed to concentrate in the memories of the past, and the condition of her former experiences were brought to view as though that lessened or atoned for her unthrift and the present carelessness of her life, and did not the rather make her more responsible to live up to those habits of neatness and cleanliness that had been taught her as a duty at that time to carry out for another.

Are we depending on past experience and position? Are we comparing ourselves with others who may not live so morally, and forgetting the greater claims upon us for our advantages?

CHAPTER 7

Eulogies

Every death provides an opportunity to reflect on the life lived, as well as the very nature of life, death, and life after death. Shipley's journal includes three eulogies for three very different lives: 16-year-old John Sensenny,[1] 27-year-old Rachel Balderston,[2] and 92-year-old Hannah Wilson.[3]

Sensenny was one of the wards at The Children's Home, an institution that Shipley founded in 1864 to place orphaned and abandoned children into families. He was born in Bloomington, Illinois, in 1857, but after his mother's death around 1866, his father threw him out and told the nine-year-old to earn his living for himself. By 1869, he found his way to Cincinnati and was brought to The Children's Home by a police officer. Although the staff at The Children's Home typically placed their youngsters in families as soon as practicable, they kept Sensenny there for a while, as he was helpful with chores. In 1872 he was situated in a home in Cumminsville, a community about six miles north of downtown Cincinnati, where he was to learn shoemaking. The problematic limb mentioned in the sermon was his leg, scalded when he was quite small.[4]

As recounted by Shipley, Sensenny's life is an archetypal story of a youngster taught well by his mother, only to fall into sin and then later find redemption. Shipley, who was clearly well-acquainted with the youth, speaks of Sensenny experiencing a "season of religious awakening," suggesting that his conversion was a gradual development rather than an instantaneous experience, but that its effects were nonetheless "distinct and positive." This eulogy is particularly powerful because Shipley was present at the boy's death, and he subsequently reflects on the contrast between the solemnity of the bedside and the vivacity of the bustling street outside the hospital. Shipley calls on his listeners to likewise reflect on death and life, specifically the idea of a death or life without Christ, and to choose one with Christ.

Shipley's brief eulogy for Balderston, whose mother was a member of Cincinnati Monthly Meeting,[5] reflects the equal regard with which Quakers held women. He speaks of her as a sparkling young person with her own strong goals, full of promise, but still needing the protection of "the shield of faith." In his message he imagines her in the afterlife, expressing words of praise and thanksgiving to God.

Shipley delivered Wilson's eulogy in Kendal, England, just as he was preparing to return to the United States.[6] Hannah Wilson was a Quaker minister herself and the mother of Robert Wilson, who helped organize the first Keswick Convention—a large religious event that occurred in Kendal during the summer of 1875, at which Shipley spoke.[7] The Keswick Convention would soon become the central institution of the holiness movement. If Shipley was not already acquainted with the Wilsons prior to that, he clearly came to know Hannah Wilson before her death. He speaks of her strength and individuality of character, her joyful and powerful ministry, and her attention to both the physical and spiritual needs of the poor, the sick, and the despondent.

In Wilson's eulogy, Shipley used more traditional Quaker language than was his custom. Here he speaks of worshiping God "in spirit and in truth," a phrase that Fox often invoked to describe Friends' tradition of silent waiting upon the Lord as opposed to the formal liturgies used by other denominations. Shipley alludes to the Quaker reliance on direct revelation when he mentions that all are "to be taught by Him, by His Spirit." He leverages frequently used Quaker metaphors when he talks of "stepping out of darkness into [God's] marvelous light," and of God as "infinite as a fountain." In this message, "the pages of divine revelation"—the scriptures—are described as an aid to help prevent people from having to "strain our eyes into the mists that surround us," a tool for discerning the truth rather than the exclusive source of all truth.

Shipley also acknowledges "the feebleness of our humanity and the frailty of our dispositions . . . the fickleness of our own love . . .

the inconstancy of our own consecration . . . our drooping energy . . . our weak faith." Here he speaks of these things not to chasten his listeners, but rather to point to God as a source of love, peace, patience, consolation, and hope.

On the Death of John Sensenny[8]

Let me die the death of the righteous, and let my last end be like his!
— NUMBERS 23:10

God has made various ties to bind together the hearts of men. The nearest is that of kindred, and this tie of blood relationships, being one of God's own creating, ought ever to be a bond to unite hearts so allied. Another—the bond of sympathy, especially where it is that sympathy that springs from fellowship in the love of the Lord Jesus Christ—has a tie of blood relationship, but it is in His blood that cleanses from all sin.

I believe both classes as true mourners are gathered here this day, who in these two varied but similar relationships mingle our grief and rejoicing around him whom we loved, and whom a loving Father in an all-wise providence has given to feel and say that to depart and to be with Christ is far better.

In [John's] life we can trace the overruling hand of Divine Providence and faith, [and] looking unto the future realize that today, He who thus watched over this young man and led him into a Christian life extends pierced hands to all to blot out past transgressions and to lift up unto newness of life that soul that is not walking with Christ.

In a conversation I had with him a few weeks ago, he spoke of the good impressions made in his mind by a mother's teaching. But the contact with sorrow and sin had blunted his moral and spiritual sensibilities. And when he became an inmate of [The Children's Home], he confessed he had lost his interest in things of a higher character than the mere needs of life and the appeals of our lower nature. A homeless boy in a large city, with relatives so near to him who, since they have known of him, have shown every recognition of that first tie of kindred-by-blood relationship—homeless [for so many years] and yet with friends so near. Dear friends, does it not speak to some of our own condition? Home means love, speaking, doing, suffering. Home means sympathy, fellowship, rest.

Are any here homeless in this higher sense, and yet kindred so near? Ah! There is one who is love, speaking, doing, suffering. He says, "I came not to call the righteous, but sinners to repentance."[9] He daily loadeth us with benefits, and while we were yet sinners, he died for us. Home means sympathy, and Christ is touched with the feeling of our infirmities. It means fellowship. He was tempted in all points like as we are. It means rest. And thou stranger in a homeland, so alone and yet so near to Him who claims thee by the tie of His own blood shed for thee, wander not homeless, friendless, lost—come to Jesus, he waits to welcome thee.

[John] stated that the influences of a Christian home (The Children's Home) reawakened and made more permanent desires for a truer, better life. And during a season of religious awakening there years ago he was brought to see himself a lost sinner, but brought to understand that Jesus Christ came to save that which was lost. His change was distinct and positive. He won the love of all hearts. "Our John" was his name, and today those connected with The Home mourn the loss of "our John." At the time of our conversation, in looking forward to the removal of his limb which from his youth had troubled him, he expressed his sense of redemption through the blood of Christ and his trust in Him.

After the most careful treatment by our most eminent surgeons, we promised ourselves many happy years of usefulness for our John, but our Lord willed to take this early ripened grain to Himself. For three days our hopes were full, but by 10 o'clock of the fourth day, unfavorable symptoms set in, and in the evening, his friends were called to his bedside.

He was perfectly conscious, [and] said about twenty minutes before he died, in answer to a remark that it would be well with him if he should not get well, "It will be better. I will see my mother and my brother. Tell the children at The Home I'm not afraid to die. And Christ has promised, 'God shall wipe away all tears from their eyes; and there shall be no more death, neither sorrow, nor crying, neither shall there be any more pain: for the former things are passed away.'"[10]

These were about his last words. A change soon came, and he fell asleep in Jesus, so peacefully, so quietly. And these last few moments, the company surrounding stood in silence. No word was spoken until his life with us was over, and when involuntarily there sprung to our lips the words which I have repeated this morning: "Let me die the death of the righteous, and let my last end be like his!"

As I passed out from by his bedside (in the Cincinnati Hospital)—from that solemn silence where death had lost its sting and the grave its victory, for he knew what it was to walk through the valley of the shadow death and fear no evil, he knew that Jesus declared Himself the resurrection and the life—I say as I passed from that solemn silence, and in a few minutes found myself in the street (Central Avenue) and heard the noise of life all around me, the wild laugh of sin, and the rush of pressing throngs, all instinct with life and preoccupied with the things that are seen, I realized our need to stop and think. Life. Death. (It is the first God wants us to choose, but not what youth calls seeing life—sin whose wages are death.) How real life seems, how it surrounds us, sweeps us along with its currents, whirls us about in its eddies, while its waters—even when dashing us on the rocks of sin—seem crested with light. And death, off in some quiet chamber, with a small group of nearest kindred or friends.[11]

We die alone unless we can claim in the shadow of death, I will fear no evil for Thou art with me.[12] To die alone, without Christ. To enter alone before the judgement seat without a mediator. Ah, my dear friends, if you would not die alone, you must not live alone. It is life Christ wants us to choose, but it is life through Him and in Him. It is passing from death of sin into life through faith in His atoning blood. It is living in union with Him, that we may die the death of the righteous.

And who is the righteous? The sinner washed in the blood of Jesus. The dying thief who says, "Lord, remember me." The repentant jailer who in response to his cry, "What must I do to be saved?" hears the answer, "Believe on the Lord Jesus Christ, and thou shalt be saved, and thy house." It is the moral centurion, Cornelius, to whom Peter preached a crucified and risen Christ. It is the persecuting Saul whom Christ meets in the way, saying, "Saul, Saul, why persecutest thou me?"[13]

Oh, by the blessed promise of Christ to the dying thief, by the joy of the forgiven jailer, by the blessed gift of the Holy Ghost to the earnestly seeking centurion, by the love and mercy and power to the persecuting Saul, I beseech thee oh sinner—choose Christ. Choose life. Flee from the wrath to come, flee to the blood that cleansth from all sin. Flee now. "I call heaven and earth to record this day against you, that I have set before you life and death, blessing and cursing: therefore choose life, that both thou and thy seed may live: that thou mayest love the Lord thy God, and that thou mayest obey his voice, and that thou mayest cleave unto him."[14]

On the Death of Rachel Balderston (Stokes)[15]

Thou hast also given me the shield of thy salvation: and thy right hand hath holden me up, and thy gentleness hath made me great.
— PSALM 18:35

For thou, Lord, wilt bless the righteous; with favor wilt thou compass him as with a shield. — PSALM 5:12

Shew thy marvellous lovingkindness, O thou that savest by thy right hand them which put their trust in thee from those that rise up against them. — PSALM 17:7

But the fruit of the Spirit is love, joy, peace, longsuffering, gentleness, goodness, faith, meekness, temperance.
— GALATIANS 5:22-23

If we could listen to the words of praise that fill the lips of her whose funeral we today attend, I think we should hear such words of thanksgiving as I have quoted. "Thou hast also given me the shield of thy salvation: and thy right hand hath holden me up, and thy gentleness hath made me great." Do you note how full of praise it is? Thou hath given—thou hath holden—thy gentleness. It is *thou* and *me*.

I well remember when she took up the shield of faith. In the brightness of her young womanhood with all the bright promises of the future, strong in her aims, she still felt the need of the protection of the shield of faith. Impressing those with whom she lived with the purity of her life and character, she saw herself in God's Light and felt the need of a purity that the blood of Christ alone gives. Looking forward to being joined in marriage, she felt the need of being joined to the Lord.

Hannah Wilson's Funeral[16]

Now the God of hope fill you with all joy and peace in believing, that ye may abound in hope, through the power of the Holy Ghost.

— ROMANS 15:13

In 2 Corinthians 13:11 we read, "the God of love and peace shall be with you." In Romans 15:5, "the God of patience and consolation grant you to be likeminded one toward another according to Christ Jesus." In Romans 15:33, "the God of peace be with you all. Amen."

Gathered before the Lord this day to worship Him in spirit and in truth, and to be taught by Him, by His Spirit, from the words of revealed truth, and in His providence that has brought us together, I ask myself and you seriously to consider some of the questions involved in this solemn occasion.

Apart from the pages of revelation, nature in her wonders marks a Creator's hand. Apart from revelation, life from death all around us—in every decaying leaf, in every seed of wheat sown in the ground—suggests a continuance of our life after death. But while thus it is true God has not left himself without a witness in that he gave us rain from heaven and fruitful seasons filling our hearts with food and gladness, yet it is equally true without the pages of divine revelation we strain our eyes into the mists that surround us. But thanks be to God—the God of love and peace, the God of patience and consolation, the God of hope—we know of the future by the appearing of Jesus Christ, who hath abolished death and brought life and immortality to light through the gospel.[17]

In France, those who commemorate the last day of their friends carry to their graves wreaths of immortelles (the type of immortality) and bunches of violets (the flower of spring and hope). And so I would join together into a triple wreath the words *hope*, *life*, and *immortality*, and in your memories lay it upon her grave who has just left us.

I would take these precious virtues of which our Lord reveals himself as God of love and peace, as God of patience and consolation, as God of hope, and while remembering them as virtues strongly marked in her character, call to your remembrance the Lord Jesus himself, the embodiment and exponent of these attributes of deity.

When the Lord would make known unto us the Father's thought towards us his rebellious children, it is love. God so loved the world he gave [his only begotten son], and in the opulence of Christ's love we readily perceive the love of God because He laid down his life for us. And God commendeth his love toward us in that while we were yet sinners [Christ died for us], but with that he couples peace. The God of love and peace. It is the salutation that Christ gives after his resurrection. When the eleven were gathered together, he stood in the midst of them and saith unto them, "Peace be unto you." It is the first message that the sinner needs to hear. It is the first right thought he needs to take of God. He needs to look up to a God of love and a Prince of Peace. He needs to believe it true. God is love, and looking up to our Prince, believe it true. He is our peace.[18]

It is the stepping out of darkness into His marvelous Light. Out of bondage unto Satan into the liberty of children of God. Out of condemnation into justification. Out of death into life. Out of a fearful looking for judgement into drawing near with a true heart in full assurance of faith, having our hearts sprinkled from an evil conscience and our bodies washed with pure water. Out of a life unto self into a life to Him, who "loved us, and washed us from our sins in His own blood."[19]

It was her testimony. It is the testimony of everyone who, with living faith in Christ, finds his own realization of peace, from love quickening to seeking the realization of the same love and peace to others.

While God is unchangeable and ever remains to be the God of love and peace, filling our hearts with joy and gladness, yet in the experience of the Christian life lived here among the trials, vicissitudes, and sorrows of life, we prove Him to be the God of patience and consolation. Not simply patience in its narrow sense as the opposite of impatience, but patience in that deeper meaning, which a parent's love feels, of constancy and perseverance. It is just such a God we heed. In the feebleness of our humanity and the frailty of our dispositions, in the fickleness of our own love and in the inconstancy of our own consecration, it is a God of patience and consolation that renews our drooping energy, revives our weak faith, cheers us on in the Christian race, and in the midst of sorrows consoles with the voice of the Holy Spirit so well named the *Comforter*. Yes, God makes ample provision for life. There is no weakness of humanity nor sorrow of life that the God of patience and consolation, who [is] the life spring of love and peace, does not supply to the trusting heart.

Still more. Whatever may be our theories, ideas, and fancies, the grave that we have stood by today and the grave that is awaiting each one of us is a fact. And as we say "dust to dust" and the natural sorrows of the heart asserts itself, but as though the clouds are swept away by the breath of the Lord, we hear the God of hope fill you with all joy and peace in believing that ye may abound in hope and the power of the Holy Ghost.[20]

Search the life of the Lord Jesus and find, if you can, the tone of His mind. Let not your hearts be troubled. Fear not. Be of good cheer. Thy brother shall rise again. Take no thought for the morrow.[21]

Hope is the flower of the root of confidence and the stalk of expectation.

The God of love, patience, consolation, hope. All such terms define God to be infinite, and infinite *as a fountain*, as self-communicating life and archetype of life. "Patience does not increase in the garden of nature, but it is God's gift and grace; God is the real Maker who creates it." "God is the source of all good things, and since he not only has them but they are his real essence:

since he does have love and omnipotence but is actually love and omnipotence." "From faith arises the enjoyment of peace and all blessed joys are *overflow* of hope."[22]

Do any feel they have sinned? It is a God of love that looks upon them. Do they feel the power of their rebellious heart? It is a God of peace who has made peace. Do they feel the instability of their own characters? It is a God of patience and perseverance. Are they crushed with the cares and sorrows of life? It is a God of comfort they have to do with. "Do any despair? It is a God of hope who commends us to hope in his mercy and takes pleasure in them that do so."[23]

May I ask some here then seriously to consider the life that has just closed? For the Lord says, ye are my witnesses.[24] With strength and individuality of character, with much of this world to make her happy, she found her peace in the blood of Christ and joy in His service. With a blessed sense of God's love in Christ Jesus, in the pardon of sin, she found the joy of a child in promoting the cause of her Father. She cast the strength of her character on the Lord's side and used her powers for the forwarding of His truth. But more, she found the poor, the sick, the needy, the sorrowing and despondent, those who stood [at the] door, [to] whom his providence and his Spirit guided her, that she might be the minister of His outward gifts for the body, His spiritual gifts of glad tidings through a crucified Savior, and His restoring gifts—her own bright buoy and faith, hope, and joy in the Holy Ghost.

But as years advanced, the infirmities of age kept her from many of these active duties. Yet was her mind free to seek the advancement of His cause and the good of others. One characteristic she was eminently endowed with: it was hope. It was hope, that confidence and expectation in it. It was a hope based in trust, and in my own interviews with her, the prevailing thought of her mind was casting all your care upon Him, for He careth for you.[25]

NOTES

In these notes, works frequently cited have been identified by the following abbreviations:

    Brinton Papers   Howard Haines Brinton and Anna Shipley Cox Brinton Papers

          CMM   Cincinnati Monthly Meeting

FOREWORD

1. A citation for this work tells its story: *The Concurrence and Unanimity of the People Called Quakers; In Owning and Asserting the Principal Doctrines of the Christian Religion; Demonstrated in the Sermons or Declarations, of Several of Their Publick Preachers, Namely, Mr. Robert Barclay, Mr. George Whitehead, Mr. John Bowater, Mr. Charles Marshall, Mr. William Bingley, Mr. John Butcher, Mr. James Park, Mr. William Dewsbery, Mr. Francis Camfield, Mr. William Penn, Mr. Richard Ashby, Mr. Samuel Waldenfield, Mr. John Vaughton, and Mr. Francis Stamper. Exactly Taken in Short-Hand, as They Were Delivered by Them in Their Meeting-Houses, in Grace-Church-Street, Devonshire-House, St. Martin's-le-Grand, St. John's-Street, Wheeler-Street, and Ratcliff, in and about London. And Now Faithfully Transcribed and Published, with the Prayer at the End of Each Sermon* (London: Nath. Crouch, 1694).

2. H. Larry Ingle, *Quakers in Conflict: The Hicksite Reformation* (Knoxville: University of Tennessee Press, 1986), 151.

PREFACE

1. Savery, *Some Remarks*, 5-6.
2. Hamm, *Transformation*, 63.
3. Hinshaw, *Encyclopedia*, Vol. V, 930; CMM Men's Minutes, May 20, 1868.
4. CMM Men's Minutes, August 20, 1874 (the sojourning minute was dated May 21, 1874, but was not added to the Meeting's records until three months later); "Late Marine Intelligence," *The Philadelphia Inquirer*, May 26, 1874, indicates that Shipley was accompanied by several of his children, as well as a cousin of his deceased wife.

5. Bownas, *Qualifications*, 48.
6. Brinton Papers, 14, 28, 30, 264 (the first two dated sermons were not the only ones out of chronological order).
7. Jay, *Autobiography*, 66.
8. Murray Shipley Memorial Minute, CMM Minutes, May 11, 1900.

INTRODUCTION

1. Jones, *The Journal of George Fox*, 155.
2. Graves, *Preaching the Inward Light*, 63.
3. Jones, *The Journal of George Fox*, 75-76.
4. Bownas, *Qualifications*, 23.
5. Hamm, *Transformation*, 8.
6. Bownas, *Qualifications*, v, 11-12, 26.
7. Graves, *Preaching the Inward Light*, 158-160, 162, 164, 168, 170-172, 176, 179.
8. Ibid., 144.
9. Bownas, *Qualifications*, 32-33.
10. Ibid., 26-28.
11. Hamm, *Transformation*, 15-16.
12. CMM Men's Preparative Meeting Minutes, June 18, 1829.
13. Hamm, *Transformation*, 15-16, 18. The names of the yearly meetings can be somewhat misleading. For example, Ohio Yearly Meeting encompassed meetings primarily in the eastern portion of the state. Many meetings in southwestern Ohio, including Cincinnati Monthly Meeting, were part of Indiana Yearly Meeting.
14. Darnowsky, *Friends Past and Present*, 23-31.
15. Hamm, *Transformation*, 20-35, 59-60.
16. Ibid., 42-45, 59.
17. Ibid., 59-60.
18. Ibid., 43.
19. Smith, *Annals*, 133-139.
20. Hinshaw, *Encyclopedia, Vol. III*, 286.
21. *A Letter, on the Dispute of Statements of Anna Braithwaite and Elias Hicks*, [9].
22. Hinshaw, *Encyclopedia, Vol. III*, 289, indicates that the entire family of Murray Shipley's mother, Sarah Shotwell, was disowned for joining the Hicksites, but that was not the case with Sarah. Before the separation she married Morris Shipley and remained with the Orthodox (Hinshaw, *Encyclopedia, Vol. III*, 286-287).

23. Hinshaw, *Encyclopedia, Vol. III*, 287 cites June 7, 1843 as the date of the Shipleys' certificate of removal from New York Monthly Meeting. However, Shipley's mother filed her will in Cincinnati on December 10, 1842, so they must have arrived sometime that year.
24. "Friends' General Meeting," *Christian Worker* 8 (September 15, 1871): 141.
25. CMM Men's Minutes, November 15, 1860.
26. Johnson, *Reminiscences*, 80-81; Hamm, *Transformation*, 60-61.
27. Hamm, *Transformation*, 76.
28. Charles F. Coffin, "Murray Shipley and Indiana Yearly Meeting of Friends," October 22, 1903, Charles F. and Rhoda M. Coffin Papers.
29. Hamm, *Transformation*, 74.
30. William Shipley Taylor to Charles, letter, December 9, 1869, Taylor Family Papers. The "close of meeting" is the end of a worship service; "1st day" is Sunday. Morris was Shipley's oldest son and about to turn 13 (Hinshaw, *Encyclopedia, Vol. V*, 931) when Taylor wrote his letter.
31. Hamm, *Transformation*, 89-90.
32. Ibid., 58-59.
33. Ibid., 123.
34. Ibid., 77.
35. Ibid., 106-107.
36. Ibid., 85, 88.
37. Darnowsky, *Friends Past and Present*, 58-61.
38. Richard G. Coleman, Chapter 8, "John Henry Douglas, Quaker Evangelist," in Snarr, *Claiming Our Past*, 57.
39. Hamm, *Transformation*, 85.
40. CMM Minutes, December 14, 1900.

CHAPTER 1 *Personal Anecdotes*

1. Bownas, *Qualifications*, 53.
2. Heiss, *Marriages from The Christian Worker*, 63.
3. Hinshaw, *Encyclopedia, Vol. V*, 909, 940. "Jenny" is a diminutive of Jane.
4. Steer, *Through Grace to Glory*, 207-208.
5. Darnowsky, *Friends Past and Present*, 284.
6. Ibid., 73.
7. Brinton Papers, 30-31.
8. Charlotte Elliott, "Just as I Am," hymn, 1835.
9. Matthew 11:28.

10. John 5:40.
11. Brinton Papers, 98.
12. MacMillan, *Bible Teachings in Nature*, 213–214.
13. Ibid., 217, 227, 230.
14. Brinton Papers, 144–145.
15. Mark 10:9.
16. Brinton Papers, 257–258.
17. Matthew 13:3–23.
18. Matthew 28:19. Shipley's parenthetical addition of *into* reflects the traditional Quaker understanding that baptism is a spiritual rather than a physical experience.
19. John 6:63.

CHAPTER 2 *Dramatic Narratives*

1. Brinton Papers, 2.
2. "Happy Effect of Christian Fidelity," *The Vermont Chronicle*, August 4, 1847; "Effect of Christian Fidelity," *The New-York Evangelist*, August 12, 1847; "What Will You Say, Sir?," *The Puritan Recorder* (Boston), March 14, 1850. In other newspaper articles unrelated to this particular anecdote, Hoopoo's name is sometimes spelled Hopoo.
3. "What Will You Say, Sir?," *Western Christian Advocate* (Cincinnati), July 31, 1850.
4. Brinton Papers, 46–48.
5. Matthew 9:1–7.
6. Matthew 8:5–13.
7. Shipley's quotations in this paragraph are from Matthew 9:2 and Matthew 9:6. Matthew 9:6 actually says "go unto thine house" rather than "walk."
8. Luke 5:28.
9. Luke 5:29.
10. This reference appeared in quotation marks in Shipley's journal, but with no attribution.
11. Mark 10:21–22 (paraphrased).
12. Luke 5:1–11; Matthew 26:56–58.
13. Brinton Papers, 60–64.
14. The context of this verse pertains to the story of friends of a man who had palsy; they brought him to a place where Jesus was performing healings.
15. "Just as they were" is likely an allusion to the hymn "Just as I Am," written by Charlotte Elliott in 1835.

16. Shipley's assertion that Jesus healed 500 individuals is his own speculation about what constituted "multitudes." According to Acts 1:15, after Jesus's ascension about 120 individuals gathered in an upper room to pray.
17. Matthew 5:3-11 (paraphrased).
18. John 6:26.
19. Matthew 7:28 (paraphrased).
20. Matthew 19:13-14.
21. Brinton Papers, 114-117.
22. Luke 2:48-49.
23. John 18:37.
24. Brinton Papers, 164-169.
25. Leviticus 8:5-34.
26. Exodus 14:31.
27. Luke 24:50-52 (paraphrased).
28. Romans 8:34.
29. Hebrews 10:19.
30. Romans 8:1 (paraphrased).
31. Brinton Papers, 37-41.
32. Luke 11:53-54.
33. Matthew 9:9-13 (paraphrased).
34. Luke 7:36-43 (paraphrased).
35. Brinton Papers, 72-74.
36. This quotation is not attributed and there is no obvious scriptural reference.
37. John 21:19; Mark 10:9; Matthew 26:58. The verse regarding what God has joined (Mark 10:9) is specific to marriage, but Shipley is applying it here in the sense of the disciples being joined to Jesus.
38. These three questions come from Mark 8:29, Matthew 26:40, and John 21:15.
39. John 20:19.
40. John 20:29.

CHAPTER 3 *Parables, Allegories, and Analogies*

1. Graves, *Preaching the Inward Light*, 184-186, 201.
2. 1876 and 1877 United States House of Representatives Elections, https://en.wikipedia.org/wiki/1876_and_1877_United_States_House_of_Representatives_elections#Election_dates, accessed February 18, 2022.
3. Murray Shipley to Sarah Murray, letter, August 3, 1850, Archives of The Shipley School.

4. Brinton Papers, 95.
5. 1 Timothy 1:15.
6. Brinton Papers, loose sheets between pages 150 and 151.
7. Isaiah 53:6.
8. Sir William Blackstone was an eighteenth-century English jurist, judge, and Tory politician famous for his lectures and writing on English law. Joseph Story served as an associate justice of the Supreme Court of the United States from 1812 to 1845 and was known for his commentaries on the U.S. Constitution.
9. Acts 22:28.
10. Genesis 1:2–3.
11. John 12:46 (paraphrased)
12. Brinton Papers, 153–156.
13. Luke 23:39–43 (paraphrased).
14. John 3:1–3, 14–15.
15. John 3:14.
16. John 3:16.
17. Ezekiel 18:4.
18. This begins as an allusion to Mark 4:3–8, but then Shipley takes it in his own direction.
19. Brinton Papers, 174–175.
20. 2 Corinthians 11:14.
21. 2 Chronicles 30:8.
22. The text suggests this is a reference to a manufacturer in Mealbank, England, just north of Kendal.
23. Romans 12:1.
24. Hopkins, *The Holy Life*, 21.
25. Brinton Papers, 234–235.
26. Brinton Papers, 234–235.
27. Matthew 25:41; Matthew 25:34.
28. Luke 16:10.
29. John 1:29 (the inclusion of "Repent!" is Shipley's addition).
30. John 12:46 (paraphrased).
31. "The Pork Ring of 1872," *Cincinnati Daily Gazette*, December 17, 1875.
32. The reference to gold here alludes to an attempt by Wall Street speculators to corner the U.S. gold market in 1869, which caused a brief financial panic. Shipley was also indicting any businesses that colluded to control the prices of goods.
33. Brinton Papers, 246–249.

34. Bengel, *Gnomon of the New Testament*, Vol. III, 215.
35. Pearson, *The Whole Works of Robert Leighton*, 130–131.
36. Ibid., 426.
37. Kempis, *The Imitation of Christ*, 80.
38. Philippians 1:21; 1 Corinthians 2:16.
39. Brinton Papers, 252–255.
40. Genesis 45:4–8.
41. John 19:9–11.
42. John 11:49–50.
43. Shipley made several errors in his original paragraph. He attributed the massacre to Charles XII rather than Charles IX, and he gave the year as 1575 rather than 1572. The quotation appears to be a paraphrase from Guizot, *History of France*, 386.
44. Psalm 37:23.
45. 1 Samuel 16:1–18 (paraphrased).
46. Psalm 20:6.
47. Numbers 14:4; Numbers 14:40.
48. Luke 15:12.
49. Luke 15:14–19 (paraphrased).
50. Proverbs 14:12; Psalm 75:7.

CHAPTER 4 *Current Events and Social Reform*

1. Sarah Murray to Murray Shipley, letter, July 23, 1863, Archives of The Shipley School.
2. Hamilton County Lease Book 42, 504–506, April 8, 1871.
3. CMM Men's Minutes, May 21, 1874.
4. CMM Men's Minutes, December 17, 1874.
5. CMM Men's Minutes, February 18, 1875.
6. Hinshaw, *Encyclopedia*, Vol. V, 931; *The Alumna*, 9.
7. *An Account of the Free-School Society of New York*, 5–6.
8. Hinshaw, *Encyclopedia*, Vol. III, 108, 286–287.
9. Hinshaw, *Encyclopedia*, Vol. III, 288–289. By the time Shipley gave this sermon, Mary Shotwell had married his father, Morris Shipley, after the death of Murray Shipley's mother (Mary Shotwell's sister), Sarah Shotwell Shipley (Hinshaw, *Encyclopedia*, Vol. V, 930).
10. "Colored Orphans, First Annual Report of the Association for the Benefit of Colored Orphans," *New-York Observer*, February 24, 1838.

NOTES: CHAPTER 4

11. Hinshaw, *Encyclopedia*, Vol. V, 931; *Memorial of Mary Jordan Taylor*.
12. Hinshaw, *Encyclopedia*, Vol. V, 902, 922; Vol. VI, 295, 307–308.
13. Darnowsky, *Friends Past and Present*, 284.
14. Brinton Papers, 51–52.
15. In Numbers 13:1-31, Moses sends men to scout out the land of Canaan, which they report as flowing with milk and honey. However, they also reported that the people of the land were strong, and their cities were walled. When Caleb encouraged the Israelites to take the land, the scouts discouraged it, saying, "We be not able to go up against the people, for they are stronger than we."
16. Psalm 71:16.
17. This is a stanza from "Not Knowing" by Mary Gardiner Brainard. The poem first appeared in the March 1869 edition of *The Congregationalist* and was set to music as a hymn by Philip Paul Bliss in the 1870s.
18. This paragraph is a quotation that Shipley attributed to Steinhofer, possibly Friedrich Christoph Steinhofer, an eighteenth-century German theologian and pietist.
19. Tyndall, *Lectures on Light*, 34. Shipley's additions to the quotation are enclosed in parentheses. The sentence between the quoted sections is Shipley's paraphrase of Tyndall's summary. Shipley enclosed the phrase "that is never severed from the factual world" in quotation marks, but it is not part of Tyndall's lectures.
20. Brinton Papers, 66–67.
21. Brinton Papers, 223–224.
22. Genesis 41:1–4 (more recent translations of the Bible refer to *kine* as *cows*).
23. James 2:20.
24. Matthew 25:21.
25. Luke 2:10.
26. Brinton Papers, 270–277.
27. Matthew 19:14; Luke 7:37–48; John 11:36.
28. John Howard was a well-known eighteenth-century prison reformer.
29. John Ashworth and John Bright were both contemporaries of Shipley. Ashworth was an English preacher who founded the Chapel for the Destitute in Rochdale, England. Bright, a Quaker, was a member of the British House of Commons and a pacifist who promoted free trade, electoral reform, and religious freedom.
30. George Müller migrated from Prussia to England in the 1830s and cared for more than 10,000 orphans during his lifetime. Adalbert von der Recke-Vomerstein likewise dedicated his life to working with orphans, particularly the handicapped and ill.

31. Luke 12:15.
32. Revelation 7:14.
33. Galatians 6:2
34. Buxton, *Memoirs of Sir Thomas Fowell Buxton*, 5.
35. 1 Peter 3:8.
36. Matthew 21:23.
37. The phrase "crippled and ruptured" referred to individuals who used a brace on their legs to walk, as well as those who used a brace to hold in organs displaced by a hernia, both of which were considered incurable conditions at the time. Shipley was likely familiar with the Hospital for the Ruptured and Crippled that was founded in New York in 1863.
38. Matthew 25:40 (paraphrased).
39. Oosterzee, *Commentary*, 423. Shipley attributed this quote to Rieger, but Oosterzee attributed it to Heubner. Oosterzee did not give the full names for either Rieger or Heubner, although Heubner was likely the German theologian Heinrich Leonhard Heubner.
40. Luke 12:34.
41. Isaiah 45:3.

CHAPTER 5 *Explications*

1. Graves, *Preaching the Inward Light*, 28; Hamm, *Transformation*, 25-26.
2. *The Catalog of St. Xavier College*, 1-2, 13; Fortin, *To See Great Wonders*, 34.
3. "Fire at Newport," *Licking Valley Register*, May 23, 1846.
4. Darnowsky, *Friends Past and Present*, 73.
5. Brinton Papers, 34-35.
6. Montagu, *Of the Proficience and Advancement of Learning*, 131.
7. Shipley inadvertently referred to Sir Roderick Murchison as Sir John Murchison.
8. Shipley's first wife, Hannah D. Taylor, was an 1850 graduate of the Wesleyan Female College in Cincinnati (*The Alumna*, 9). His youngest daughter, Katharine M. Shipley, would graduate from the same institution in 1877 (*The Alumna*, 9) and would in 1890 be a member of the first graduating class of Bryn Mawr. She and two of Shipley's other daughters went on to found The Shipley School, a young ladies' preparatory school (Vaux, *A Daring Vision*, 12-13).
9. Froude, *Inaugural Address*, 23.
10. Miss Faithful is a reference to Emily Faithful, an English advocate for women's suffrage, employment, and education. She founded a printing establishment for women called The Victoria Press, which published the feminist *English Woman's Journal* and later the monthly *Victoria Magazine*. This quotation

NOTES: CHAPTER 5

may have appeared in one of those publications, although Faithful also wrote for other newspapers and magazines.

11. Isaiah 45:11.
12. "Morte D'Arthur," Alfred Lord Tennyson. It is uncertain which book of Tennyson's poems Shipley had.
13. Ecclesiastes 7:12.
14. Brinton Papers, 68–70.
15. John 14:27.
16. Exodus 33:16.
17. Exodus 33:15; Psalm 10:4.
18. 1 Kings 19:9.
19. Romans 8:28; 1 Peter 5:7; Matthew 28:20.
20. Brinton Papers, 92–93.
21. *Sermons Preached at Trinity Chapel*, 296.
22. Psalm 89:14 (Shipley inverts the order of the psalmist, who began with justice and judgement and ended with mercy and truth); Exodus 34:6-7; Habakkuk 1:13.
23. Shipley treats "who was God manifest . . . shall reveal him" as a single quotation. Although there are snippets of scripture in this quotation, it is not entirely Biblical text. He might be quoting Robertson or Liddon here.
24. Hebrews 7:26; John 8:46.
25. Matthew 4:1-11; Luke 11:53-54; 1 Peter 2:22.
26. Liddon, *Some Elements of Religion*, 227 (Shipley used "sins" rather than "trespasses").
27. Ibid., 161 (parenthetical added by Shipley), 215 (emphasis added by Shipley), 207 (the original text phrases it as a question—"Is He, in short"—but Shipley transposes the words for this quotation).
28. Mark 9:43; Mark 14:21.
29. Brinton Papers, 100–101.
30. John 9:31.
31. Romans 5:7; Matthew 5:44; Matthew 5:46.
32. Luke 23:34.
33. Shipley wrote the name Des Lewis in this paragraph.
34. 1 Corinthians 15:3; Galatians 2:20.
35. Logan, *Sermons, Lectures, and Communion Service*, 221.
36. Brinton Papers, 109–111.
37. Romans 8:25.
38. Psalm 39:7.

39. Brinton Papers, 230–233.
40. "Under some measure of Light" is a Quaker expression that indicates some portion of divine revelation. Friends generally believe that only Jesus had "a full measure of Light." The previous sermon that Shipley alludes to here is *Tribulation*, which appears in Chapter 4.
41. The previous week's sermon, *Obedience of Faith*, appeared in Shipley's journal but is not included in this book.
42. John 6:38.
43. Matthew 7:20.
44. Jeremiah 17:5–6.
45. Ruth 2:12; Psalm 25:2; Psalm 125:1; Isaiah 50:10; Matthew 12:21.
46. Romans 10:17; Mark 1:15; Romans 5:1; Romans 3:28.
47. John 5:30.
48. Acts 13:39.
49. Matthew 18:3.
50. Hare, *The Victory of Faith*, 38.
51. Ibid., 51.
52. Ibid., 51–52.
53. Brinton Papers, 278–281, 4. At the end of page 281, Shipley added a pointer to page 4, an earlier page in the journal that he had not previously written on.
54. 1 Corinthians 2:14 (paraphrased); Fronmüller, *The Epistles General of Peter* (2007 edition), 40.
55. 1 Corinthians 3:10.
56. Jean Goujon (which Shipley misspelled Gougon) was a sixteenth-century French renaissance sculptor. Bernard Palissy did not in fact die during the Saint Bartholomew's Day Massacre in 1572. His life was likely spared by Catherine de' Medici, as he was a personal favorite of hers.
57. Hebrews 6:10.

CHAPTER 6 *Exhortation*

1. Bownas, *Qualifications*, vi.
2. Barclay, *Apology*, 18.
3. *The Discipline of the Society of Friends*, 38, 40, 41.
4. Mary Shipley Mills, "A Goodly Heritage," *The Shipley School News Letter*, Bryn Mawr, Pennsylvania, Fall 1948.
5. Bownas, *Qualifications*, 55. Bownas was speaking here specifically about a minister's potential reaction to not receiving approval from his Meeting to

NOTES: CHAPTER 6

travel in ministry, but the principle of not reacting badly to negative feedback can be universally applied.

6. CMM Men's Minutes, August 20, 1874 (the sojourning minute that Shipley received from Cincinnati Monthly Meeting was dated May 21, 1874, but was not added to the meeting's records until three months later).
7. *Obituary Record of Yale Graduates*, 361; Dillingham, *A History of the Class of '82*, 375.
8. Woolman, *The Journal of John Woolman*, 192.
9. *Second Annual Report of the Associated Executive Committee of Friends on Indian Affairs*.
10. Brinton Papers, 76–79.
11. Mark 12:30.
12. Psalm 37:31; Psalm 40:8; Psalm 119:11; Psalm 119:98.
13. Mark 12:32–34.
14. Romans 13:10 (although this phrase was written by the Apostle Paul, Shipley attributes the sentiment here to Jesus); John 21:15; Mark 8:29; Matthew 26:40–41.
15. The first quote (which Shipley did not attribute) is from the French Abbot Bernard of Clairvaux. The second he attributed to Burkitt, possibly the biblical expositor William Burkitt.
16. Clarke, *The Holy Bible, Including the Marginal Readings and Parallel Texts*, Vol. I, The Fifth Book of Moses Called Deuteronomy, Chapter 6, 462.
17. John 19:26–27.
18. Acts 1:14.
19. Exodus 20:2; Deuteronomy 6:3.
20. Brinton Papers, 127–128.
21. Romans 1:15.
22. Galatians 6:14; Romans 1:17.
23. Brinton Papers, loose sheets between pages 180 and 181.
24. 1 Corinthians 12:13; John 3:3; Luke 13:3.
25. Luke 17:27–29.
26. Romans 3:20 (paraphrased); Galatians 3:22.
27. John 16:7–9 (paraphrased); Romans 11:32.
28. Brinton Papers, 264–265.
29. Matthew 3:2, 7. "Professor" here refers to someone who professes belief.
30. Matthew 3:6.
31. Luke 15:18; 2 Samuel 12:13; Luke 18:13.
32. Matthew 3:8.

NOTES: CHAPTERS 6-7

33. Psalm 23:4.
34. Bonar, *The Works of Rev. Robert Murray McCheyne*, 160.

CHAPTER 7 **Eulogies**

1. *Temporary Children 1864–1877*, 63. Sensenny (which Shipley misspelled in his journal as "Sensensenny" and which *Temporary Children* spelled multiple ways) was born on August 7, 1857. There is no date for Shipley's eulogy, but it was delivered between November 1873 and July 1874, so Sensenny was presumably about sixteen years old.
2. "Died," *The Sun* (Baltimore, Maryland), March 24, 1874.
3. *The Annual Monitor for 1876*, 166–173.
4. *Temporary Children 1864–1877*, 63.
5. The CMM minutes indicate that Lydia Stokes was received into membership at her request on April 14, 1870. They do not indicate that her husband, Samuel Stokes, was a member. However, his obituary ("Death of Samuel Stokes, Jr.," *Cincinnati Times and Chronicle*, July 10, 1871) identifies him as a Quaker, so he may have attended even if he did not become a member. There is no record of their daughter Rachel being a member. In addition, the CMM membership records indicate that John and Rachel Balderston's daughter Lydia Ray Balderston, who was born on July 9, 1873, was received into membership on July 16, 1874 at the request of her father and grandmother.
6. CMM Men's Minutes, October 21, 1875 includes the text from a letter received from Kendal Monthly Meeting dated June 24, 1875, indicating that Shipley was "about to leave us."
7. *The Annual Monitor for 1876*, 166–173; *The Annual Monitor for 1906*, 149–153; Stevenson, *Keswick's Authentic Voice*, 16, 258.
8. Brinton Papers, 83–85.
9. Mark 2:17.
10. Revelation 21:4.
11. 1 Corinthians 15:55; Psalm 23:4; John 11:25; Romans 6:23.
12. Psalm 23:4.
13. Luke 23:42; Acts 16:30–31; Acts 10:1–48; Acts 9:4.
14. Deuteronomy 30:19–20.
15. Brinton Papers, 112. Shipley's journal misspelled her married name as "Balderson."
16. Brinton Papers, 187–190.
17. Acts 14:17; 2 Timothy 1:10.
18. John 3:16; Romans 5:8; John 20:26; Ephesians 2:14.

NOTES: CHAPTER 7

19. Hebrews 10:27; Revelation 1:5.
20. Genesis 3:19; Romans 15:13.
21. John 11:23; Matthew 6:34.
22. Shipley attributed the "patience" quote to Mueller, possibly the evangelist George Müller who operated an orphanage in Bristol, England; he attributed the "source" quote to Gerlach, possibly the German theologian Hermann Gerlach; he attributed the "faith" quote to Heubner, possibly the German theologian Heinrich Leonhard Heubner.
23. Shipley attributed this quote to Burkitt, possibly the biblical expositor William Burkitt.
24. Isaiah 43:10.
25. 1 Peter 5:7.

BIBLIOGRAPHY

Murray Shipley's Bibliography

In addition to the King James Version of the Bible, the following are works quoted by Shipley in his sermons.

Bengel, John Albert. *Gnomon of the New Testament, Vol. III.* Edinburgh: T. & T. Clark, 1858.

Bonar, Andrew A. *The Works of Rev. Robert Murray McCheyne.* New York: Robert Carter & Brothers, 1874.

Buxton, Charles, ed. *Memoirs of Sir Thomas Fowell Buxton, Baronet, with Selections from His Correspondence.* London: John Murray, 1848.

Clarke, Adam. *The Holy Bible, Containing the Old and New Testaments: The Text Printed from the Most Correct Copies of the Present Authorized Translation, Including the Marginal Readings and Parallel Texts with a Commentary and Critical Notes Designed as a Help to a Better Understanding of the Sacred Writings.* Baltimore: John J. Harrod, 1834.

Fronmüller, G. F. C. *The Epistles General of Peter,* Translated by J. Isidor Mombert. New York: Charles Scribner and Co., 1870 (Reprinted Eugene, OR: Wipf and Stock Publishers, 2007).

Froude, James Anthony. *Inaugural Address Delivered to the University of St. Andrew's, March 19, 1869.* London: Longmans, Green, and Co., 1869.

Guizot, M. (François). *A Popular History of France from the Earliest Times, Vol. IV,* Translated by Robert Black. Boston: Dana Estes and Charles E. Lauriat, [1869].

Guthrie, Thomas et. al. *Autobiography of Thomas Guthrie, D. D. and Memoir by His Sons Rev. David K. Guthrie and Charles J. Guthrie, M.A. In Two Volumes. I.* New York: Robert Carter and Brothers, 1874.

Hare, Julius Charles. *The Victory of Faith.* London: Macmillan and Co., 1874.

Hopkins, Rev. Evan H. *The Holy Life.* London: S.W. Partridge & Co, 1875.

Kempis, Thomas A. *The Imitation of Christ in Three Books*. Boston: Lincoln & Edmands, 1829.

Liddon, H. P. *Some Elements of Religion: Lent Lectures 1870*. London: Rivingtons, 1872.

Logan, John. *Sermons, Lectures, and Communion Service According to the Usage of the Church of Scotland*. Edinburgh: James Robertson, 1821.

MacMillan, Hugh. *Bible Teachings in Nature*. London: MacMillan and Co., 1871.

Montagu, B., ed. *Of the Proficience and Advancement of Learning by Francis Lord Verulam*. London: William Pickering, 1840.

Oosterzee, J. J. Van. *Theological and Homiletical Commentary on the Gospel of St Luke. Specially Designed and Adapted for the Use of Ministers and Students. From the German of J. J. Van Oosterzee, D. D. Edited by J. P. Lange, D. D., Professor of Divinity in the University of Bonn. Translated by Sophia Taylor. Volume I*. Edinburgh: T. & T. Clark, 1862.

Pearson, John Norman. *The Whole Works of Robert Leighton, D. D., Archbishop of Glasgow*. New York: J. C. Riker, 1847.

Pond, Enoch. *A History of God's Church from its Origin to the Present Time*. Philadelphia: Ziegler & McCurdy, 1871.

Sermons Preached at Trinity Chapel, Brighton, by the Late Rev. Frederick W. Robertson, M. A., The Incumbent. Third Series. Second American, from the Third London Edition. Boston: Ticknor and Fields, 1859.

Tyndall, John. *Lectures on Light: Delivered in the Unites States in 1872–73*. New York: D. Appleton and Company, 1873.

The Author's Bibliography
Books and Pamphlets

An Account of the Free-School Society of New York. New York: Collins and Co., 1814.

The Alumna: Published by the Alumnae of the Cincinnati Wesleyan Female College, 1890–1900. Cincinnati: Western Methodist Book Concern Press, 1901.

The Annual Monitor for 1876, or Obituary of the Members of the Society of Friends in Great Britain and Ireland, for the Year 1875. London: Sold by Samuel Harris and Co., 1875.

BIBLIOGRAPHY

The Annual Monitor for 1906, or Obituary of the Members of the Society of Friends in Great Britain and Ireland, for the Year 1905. London: Sold by Headley Bros., 1905.

Barclay, Robert. *An Apology for the True Christian Divinity: Being an Explanation and Vindication of the Principles and Doctrines of the People Called Quakers.* Providence, RI: Knowles and Vose, 1840.

Bownas, Samuel. *A Description of the Qualifications Necessary to a Gospel Minister.* London: W. & F. G. Cash, 1853 (originally printed in 1750).

Darnowsky, Sabrina. *Friends Past and Present: The Bicentennial History of Cincinnati Friends Meeting (1815–2015).* Printed by CreateSpace, An Amazon.com Company, 2015.

Dillingham, Edwin Lynde. *A History of the Class of '82: Yale College 1878–1910.* New York: The De Vinne Press, 1911.

The Discipline of the Society of Friends, of Indiana Yearly Meeting. Richmond, IN: E. Morgan and Sons, 1864.

Fortin, Roger A. *To See Great Wonders: A History of Xavier University, 1831–2006.* Scranton: University of Scranton Press, 2006.

Graves, Michael P. *Preaching the Inward Light: Early Quaker Rhetoric.* Waco: Baylor University Press, 2009.

Hamm, Thomas D. *The Transformation of American Quakerism: Orthodox Friends, 1800–1907.* Bloomington and Indianapolis: Indiana University Press, 1988.

Heiss, Jane R. *Marriages from the Christian Worker: A Quaker Periodical, 1871–1894 (Vol. 24).* Provo, UT: Ancestry.com Operations, Inc., 2013.

Hinshaw, William Wade. *Encyclopedia of American Quaker Genealogy.* Baltimore: Genealogical Publishing Co., Inc., 1991.

Jay, Allen. *Autobiography of Allen Jay (1831–1910).* Richmond, IN: Friends United Press, 2010.

Johnson, Mary Coffin, ed. *Rhoda M. Coffin: Her Reminiscences, Addresses, Papers and Ancestry.* New York: The Grafton Press, 1910.

Jones, Rufus M., ed. *The Journal of George Fox.* Richmond, IN: Friends United Press, 1976 (Reprinted from the 1908 edition).

A Letter, on the Dispute of Statements of Anna Braithwaite and Elias Hicks. Said to Have Been Written by Ann Shipley. Reprinted from the New-York Edition with a Review of the Same. Philadelphia: 1824.

BIBLIOGRAPHY

Obituary Record of Yale Graduates 1924–1925. New Haven, CT: Yale University, 1925.

Savery, William. *Some Remarks on the Practice of Taking Down and Publishing the Testimonies of Ministering Friends: Addressed to the Members of the Religious Society of Friends*. London: James Phillips and Son, 1797.

Second Annual Report of the Associated Executive Committee of Friends on Indian Affairs. Philadelphia: Sherman & Co., Printers, 1871.

Smith, Henry Ecroyd. *Annals of Smith of Cantley, Balby, and Doncaster, County York*. Yorkshire, England: Hills and Company, 1878.

Snarr, D. Neil and Associates. *Claiming Our Past: Quakers in Southwest Ohio and Eastern Tennessee*. Sabina, OH: Gaskins Printing, 1992.

Steer, S. R. *Through Grace to Glory: Memory Sketches from the Life of Harriet Steer*. Concord, NH: Edward A Jenks, 1887.

Stevenson, Herbert F., ed. *Keswick's Authentic Voice: Sixty-Five Dynamic Addresses Delivered at the Keswick Convention, 1875–1957*. Grand Rapids, MI: Zondervan Publishing House, 1959.

Vaux, Trina. *A Daring Vision: A History of The Shipley School, 1894–2018*. Printed in Canada: The Shipley School, 2019.

Woolman, John. *The Journal of John Woolman, With an Introduction by John G. Whittier*. Boston: James R. Osgood and Company, 1871.

Manuscripts and Other Documents

Cincinnati Friends Meeting, Cincinnati, OH
    Memorial of Mary Jordan Taylor.

Cincinnati History Library and Archives, Cincinnati, OH
    Children's Home of Cincinnati Records, Mss. 532, Box 13, Vol. 22, *Temporary Children 1864–1877*.

Earlham College, Friends Collection and College Archives, Richmond, Indiana
    Charles F. and Rhoda M. Coffin Papers.

Haverford College, Quaker & Special Collections, Haverford, Pennsylvania
    Howard Haines Brinton and Anna Shipley Cox Brinton Papers, HC.MC-1189, Box 44, Murray Shipley Manuscripts folder.
    William H. Jenks Collection.
    Taylor Family Papers, HC.MC-962, Box 6.

BIBLIOGRAPHY

The Shipley School Archives, Bryn Mawr, Pennsylvania
Shipley Family Correspondence, 1842–1900.

Wilmington College, Watson Library, Wilmington, OH
Cincinnati Monthly Meeting Men's Preparative Meeting Minutes, 1814–1893.
Cincinnati Monthly Meeting Men's Minutes, 1853–1863, 1863–1873.
Cincinnati Monthly Meeting Membership Records, Vol. 1 (1849–1918) and Vol. 2 (1850–1918).

Xavier University, University Archives and Special Collections, Cincinnati, OH
The Catalogue of St. Xavier College, Cincinnati, Ohio, for the Academical Year 1845–6. Cincinnati: Henry Gregory, Printer, 1846.

ACKNOWLEDGEMENTS

Although writing and editing might be solitary activities, a book like this cannot be completed without the assistance of others. I have many to thank, first and foremost Sarah Horowitz and the staff of the Quaker & Special Collections at Haverford College, where Shipley's journal resides. In addition to providing in-person access to their manuscript collection at the beginning of my research, during the COVID-19 pandemic they generously offered scanning services and other assistance for remote research.

I must also thank Sarah Staples of the Cincinnati History Library and Archives for her assistance in finding information about John Sensenny; Lee Bowman, Elizabeth House, and the former librarian Patti Kinsinger of the Watson Library at Wilmington College for providing access to the minute books and other records of Cincinnati Monthly Meeting; Tim McCabe of Xavier University for supplying records about Shipley's formal education; and Trina Vaux and the staff at The Shipley School for sharing with me their collection of Shipley family correspondence.

Shipley's handwriting was sometimes difficult to decipher, and I am grateful to the members of the r/Koine and r/Handwriting subreddits who examined the images I posted and provided me with their insights.

When Shipley did not provide citations for his scripture references, I was glad to be able to search the King James Version of the Bible using biblegateway.com. And when I needed to find the source for an obscure quotation, I was amazed at the extent of the digitized material provided by hathitrust.org, archive.org, and books.google.com.

I am deeply indebted to those individuals who kindly read my early drafts or otherwise provided feedback and advice: Jeff Arnold, Brent Bill, Paul Buckley, Tom Hamm, Theresa Marchwinski, Don

ACKNOWLEDGEMENTS

Ulin, and most especially Chris Pitt Lewis. I am particularly grateful to Tom Hamm for also writing the excellent foreword to this work.

My sincere gratitude goes to the staff and associates of Friends United Press, especially Dan Kasztelan for believing in the value of this work, Kristna Evans for her excellent editorial feedback, David Botwinik for his outstanding book design, and Shari Veach for shepherding this work through the production process.

And last but not least, I must thank my husband, Alan Darnowsky, for all his support as I dedicated my time to this work.

INDEX

Allegories
    Cave of the Winds, 54
    deep sea diver, 4
    foundation of sand, 83
    gondolier, 48
    ill man, 39
    keeping an object near, 2
    learning to write, 41
    lost in the woods, 2
    mill, 42
    nearsightedness, 44
    plants, 3–4, 49–50
    sheep and shepherd, 29–30
    smallpox, 6
    weighing gold, 42
Altar, family, 86, 89–90
Analogies
    borrowed land and outward virtues, 37–38
    Claude Lorraine glass and seeing Jesus, 2
    earthly and heavenly citizenship, 36–37
    love toward loved ones and enemies, 74–75
    national borders and borders of sin, 43
    unpolished stone and crude thoughts, 85
Anecdotes
    Bank of England, 42
    Cave of the Winds, 54
    estranged spouses, 4–5
    lost in the woods, 2
    sailing, 4
    seed experiment, 6
    visitations, 2, 6, 96
Appearances, 56, 96
Atonement, xvii, 8, 18, 23, 101
Balderston, Rachel, 97–98, 102–103
Baptism
    early Quaker preaching, xvi
    of Murray Shipley, 52
    references in Shipley's sermons, 6, 46, 51, 55, 66, 84
Bible
    authority of, xviii
    early Quaker preaching, xvi
    source of division, xvii
    study of, xviii
    verses in Shipley's sermons, xiii
Born again, 37, 39, 94
Bownas, Samuel, 1, 86–87
Catholicism, 84
Children's Home, xxii, 52, 97, 99–100
Civil War, 56
Communion, xvi, 46, 52
Confession, xx, xxi, 90, 95
Conversion, xxii, 39, 80
    explication, 37, 41
    of a young woman, 24–25
    of Matthew the disciple, 10–12
    of Murray Shipley, xix
Current events
    election, 36
    Long Depression, 52
    Panic of 1873, 51
    price fixing, 43
Death, 27, 49, 84, 96, 101
Doubts, 70, 85
Douglas, John Henry, xxii–xxiii
Ecumenism, x, xviii

INDEX

Education
  of early Quaker ministers, xv
  of Murray Shipley, 64
  of women, 67
Eulogies, 97–107
Evangelism, xix
Fox, George, xv, 60
Grace, xx
Great commandments, 88–89
Gurney, Joseph John, xvii, 64
Healing, 13, 15
Hicks, Elias, xvii, xix
Hicksite Separation, xvii
Holiness, 72
  preachers, xxii–xxiii
  preaching, xx
  tenets, xxi
Hoopoo, Thomas, 9, 30
Human nature, xxi–xxii
Hymns, xxiii, 3
Jay, Allen, xi
Justification, xviii, 32, 66, 94, 104
Keswick Convention, 98
Light
  inward, xv, xxi–xxii
  measure of, xv, 77
  walking in the, 22
Maxims, 16, 57
Minister, recording, xv
Mysticism, 79
New birth, 37, 39, 94
New man, 85
Novels, 24, 68
Obedience, 77, 79
Old man, 85
Ordinances. *See* Baptism, Communion.
Ordination, xv, 66, 84
Orthodox Quakerism, xvii
Parables
  prodigal son, 27, 50
  stony ground, 40–41

Plainness, xvi, xxiv, 66, 84
Politics, 57, 59
Prayer
  at family altar, 90
  outward form, 46
  power of, 68
Preaching
  direct revelation, xv
  holiness, xx
  impromptu, xi, 1
  lectionary, xv
  Quaker peculiarities, xviii
  Quaker themes in, xvi
  role of listeners, xvi
  use of scriptures, xvi
  written records, ix, x
Premillennialism, xxi–xxii, 52
Recording, ministers, xv
Repentance, 94–95
Revivals, xx–xxi
Salvation, xx–xxi, 24, 79, 101
Sanctification, xviii, xxi–xxii
Savery, William, ix
Scriptures, 20, 103
Second Coming, xxii, 52
Sensenny, John, 97, 99–102
Sermons, Shipley's. *See also* Preaching.
  dates, xi
  editorial changes to, xiii
  locations, x, xi
  reusing, xi
  times, x–xi
  titles, xiii
Shipley, Ann, xix
Shipley, Murray
  biography, xix–xx
  conversion of, xix
  journal, x, xii
  recording of, xx
Silent worship, xv, xvii, xxiii–xxiv
Singing. *See* Hymns.
Slavery, 43, 48, 59, 61

INDEX

Spirituality, 79
Stokes, Rachel. *See* Balderston, Rachel.
Temperance, 52, 60, 62–63, 66, 75
The Children's Home. *See* Children's Home.
Western European perspective, 87
Willfullness, 41, 79
Wilson, Hannah, 97–98, 103–107
Yearly meetings, xvii

ABOUT SABRINA DARNOWSKY

Sabrina Darnowsky is the author of *Friends Past and Present: The Bicentennial History of Cincinnati Friends Meeting (1815–2015)*, and her articles on Quaker research have appeared in *Friends Journal* and *Ohio Genealogy News*.

She served as a panelist at the Quaker Genealogy & History Conference on "The Life and Times of Levi Coffin," and has spoken on Quaker history, faith, and practice at multiple Cincinnati venues, including the public radio station WVXU, the Heritage Village Museum, and the Festival of Faiths. She was also a featured speaker in the award-winning documentary *Quakers: That of God in Everyone*.

She is currently writing a biography of Murray Shipley.

ABOUT THOMAS D. HAMM

Thomas D. Hamm is an Emeritus Professor of History at Earlham College, and for many years curated the Friends Collection and College Archives there. He is the author of several books, including *The Transformation of American Quakerism: Orthodox Friends, 1800–1907*.

www.ingramcontent.com/pod-product-compliance
Lightning Source LLC
Chambersburg PA
CBHW032259150426
43195CB00008BA/515